COLOURING FUN FOR EVERYONE

Colouring and Join the Dots

By
Ruth Irwin

Copyright © 2019 Ruth Irwin. All rights reserved.
Produced by Amazon Digital Services
ISBN: 9781670548016

All drawings and pictures used within this book have been drawn by the author.
Copyright © 2019 Ruth Irwin. All rights reserved.

PLEASE NOTE: IDENTICAL DRAWINGS ARE USED IN TWO COLOURING BOOKS BY RUTH IRWIN: "COLOURING FUN FOR EVERYONE" AND "COLOURING DELIGHTS WITH POETIC INSIGHT."

COLOURING FUN FOR EVERYONE

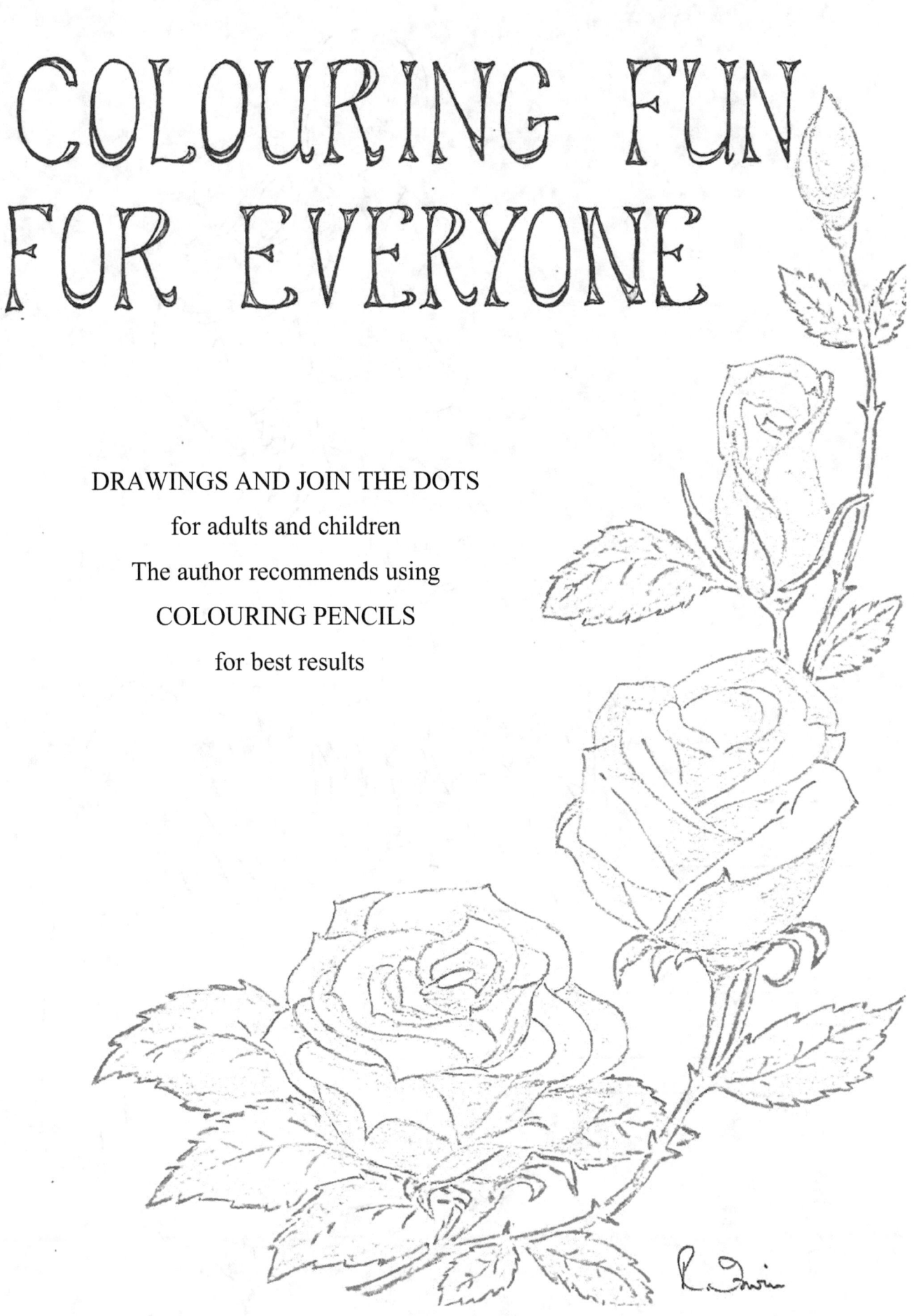

DRAWINGS AND JOIN THE DOTS

for adults and children

The author recommends using

COLOURING PENCILS

for best results

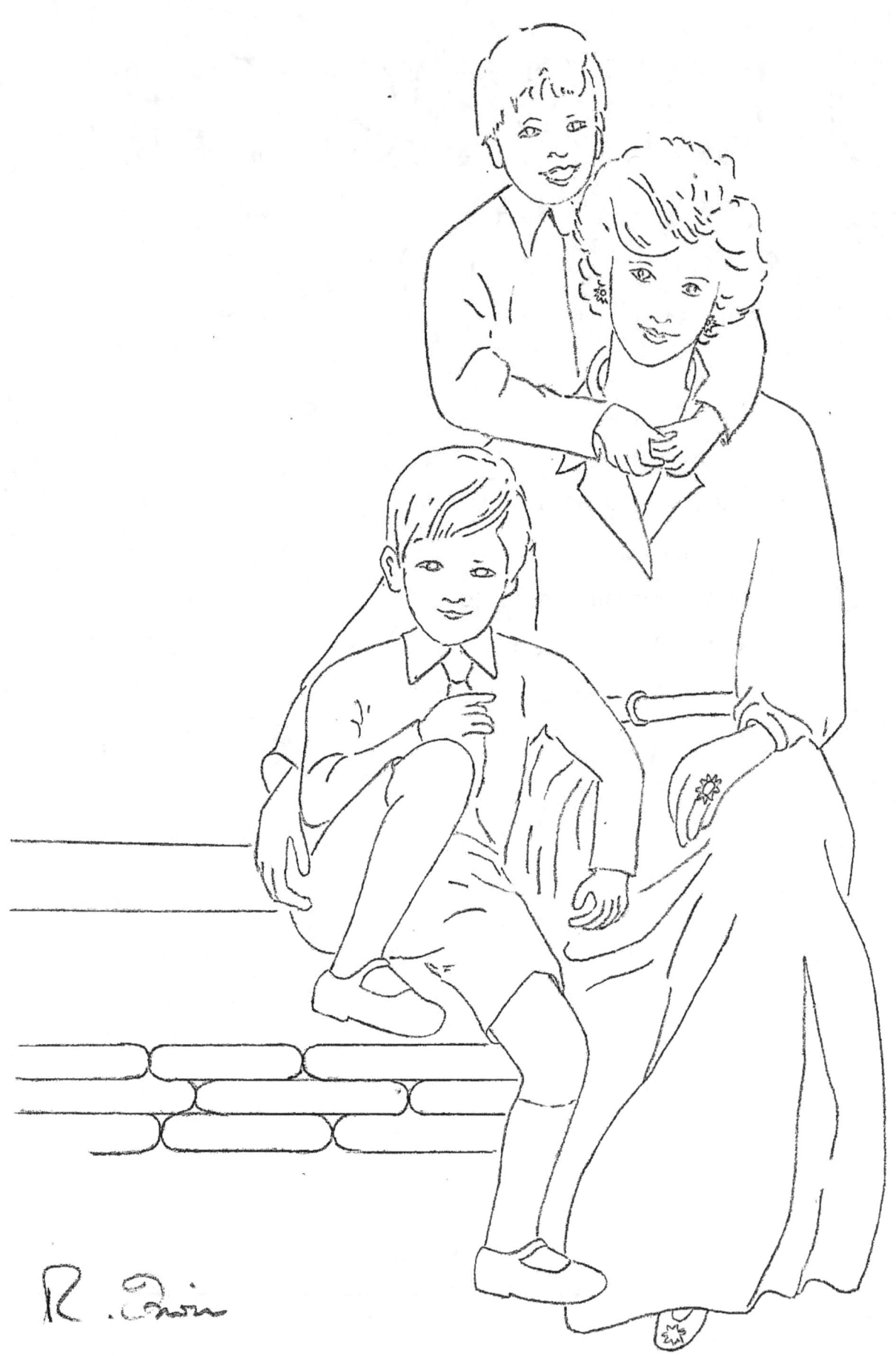

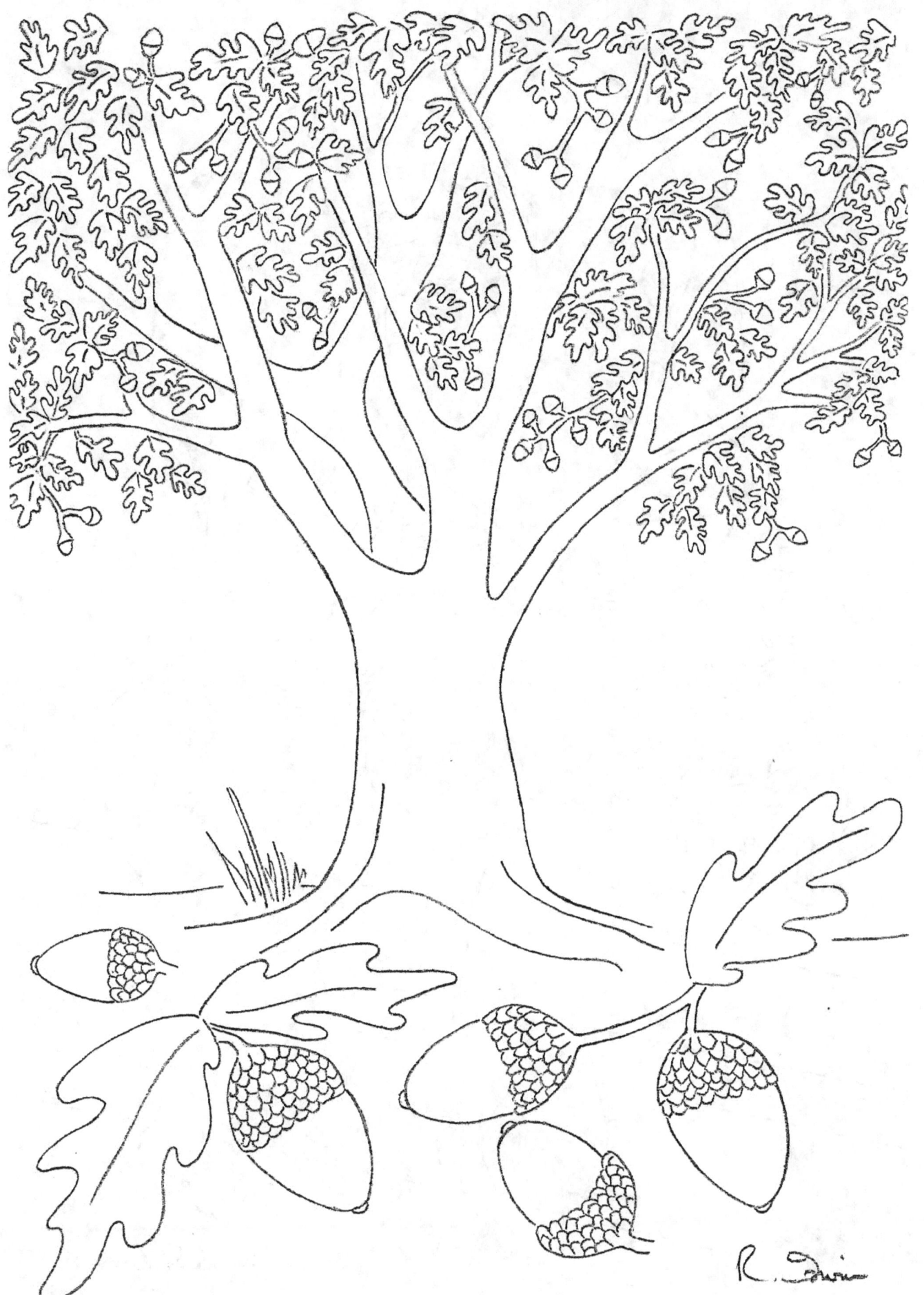

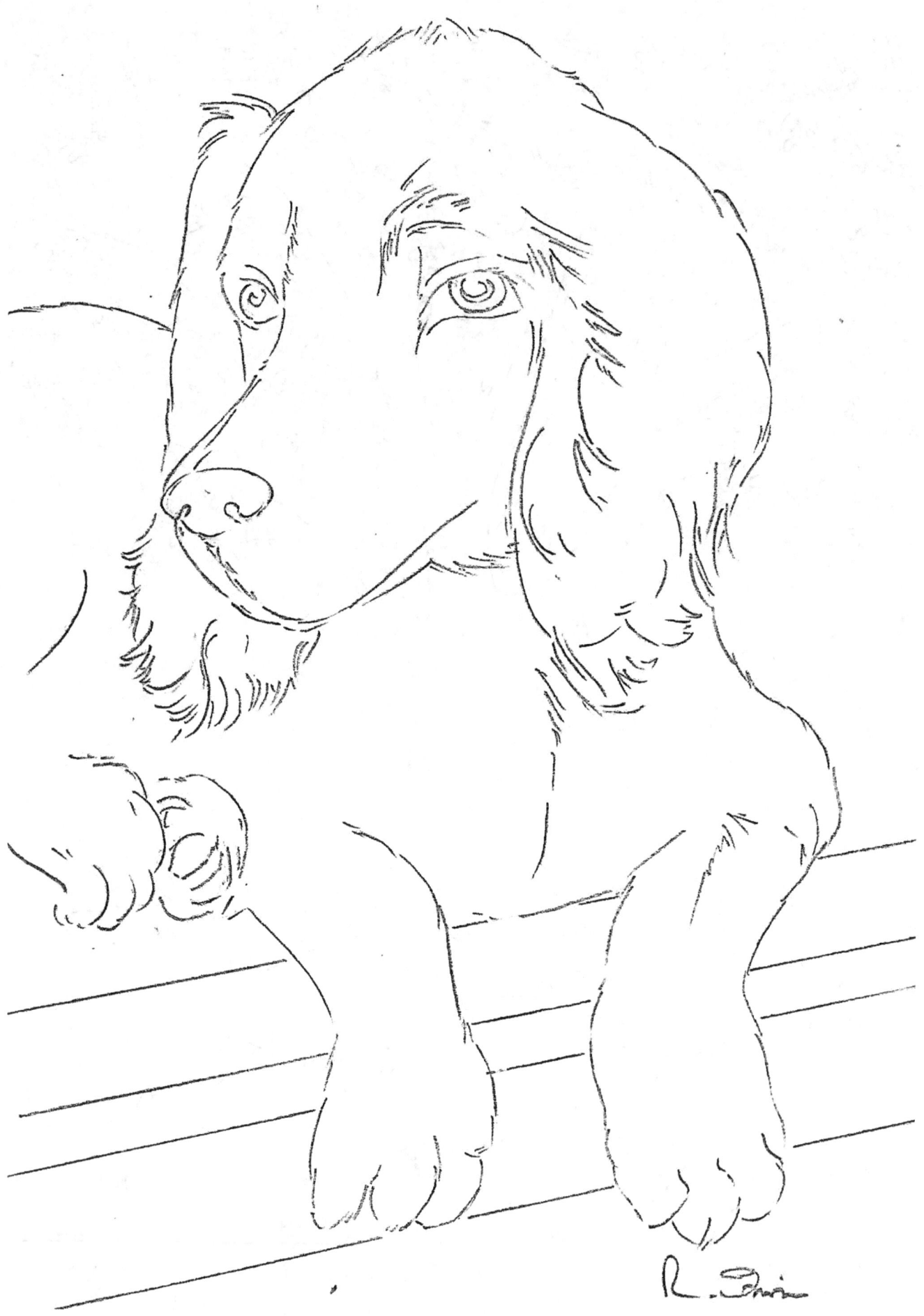

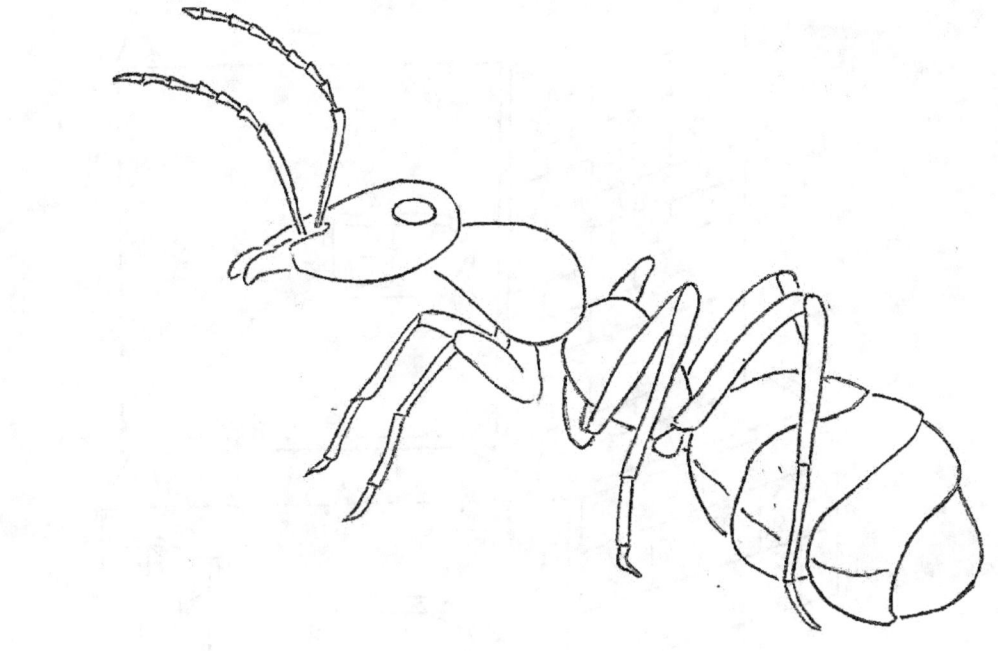
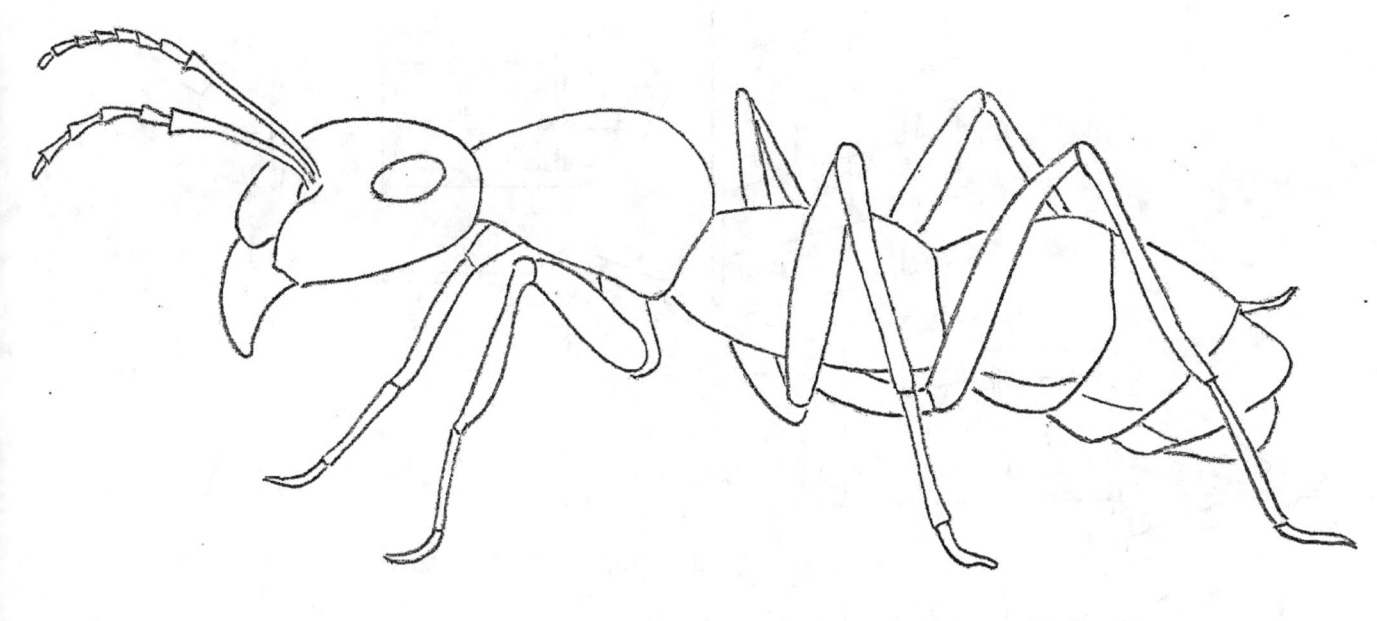

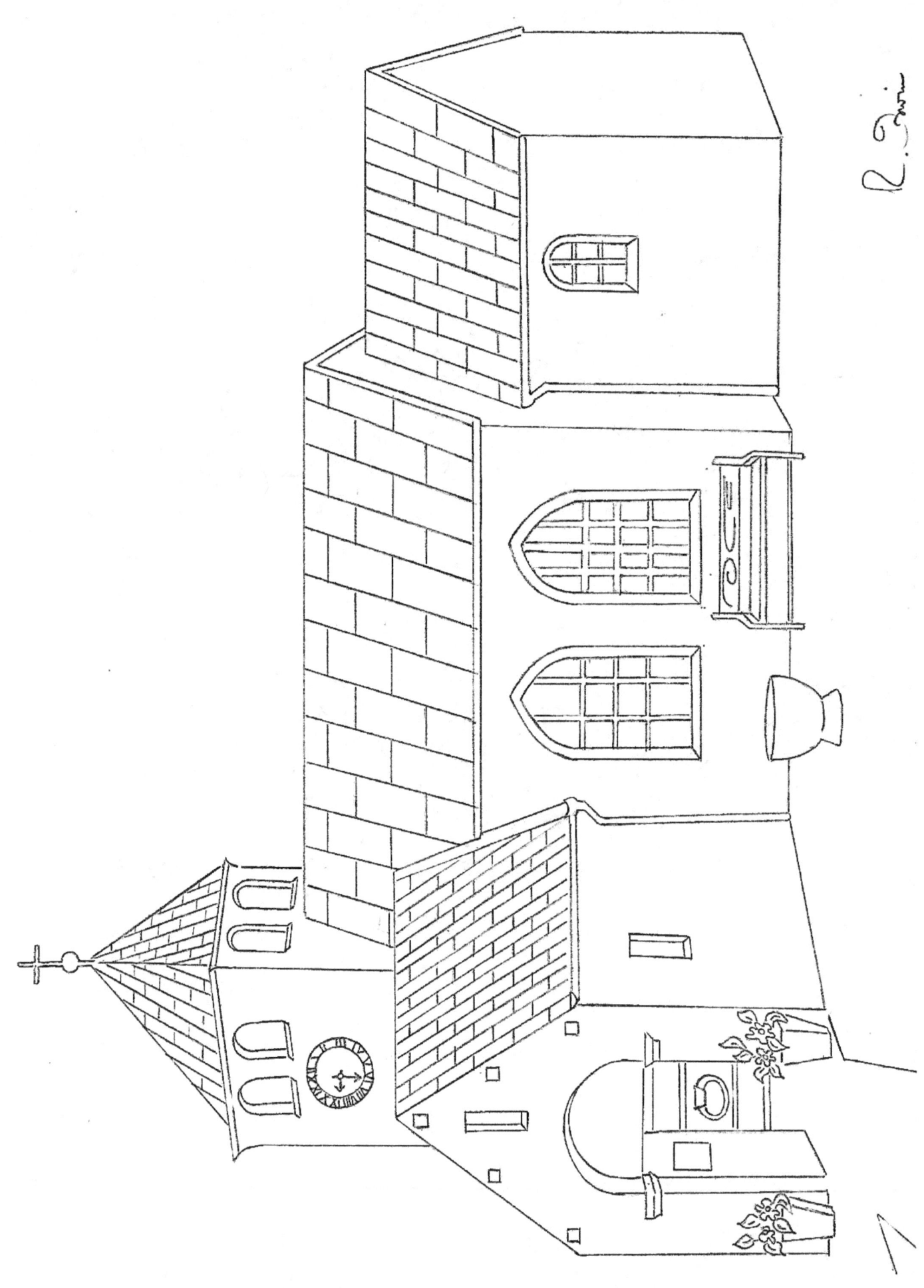

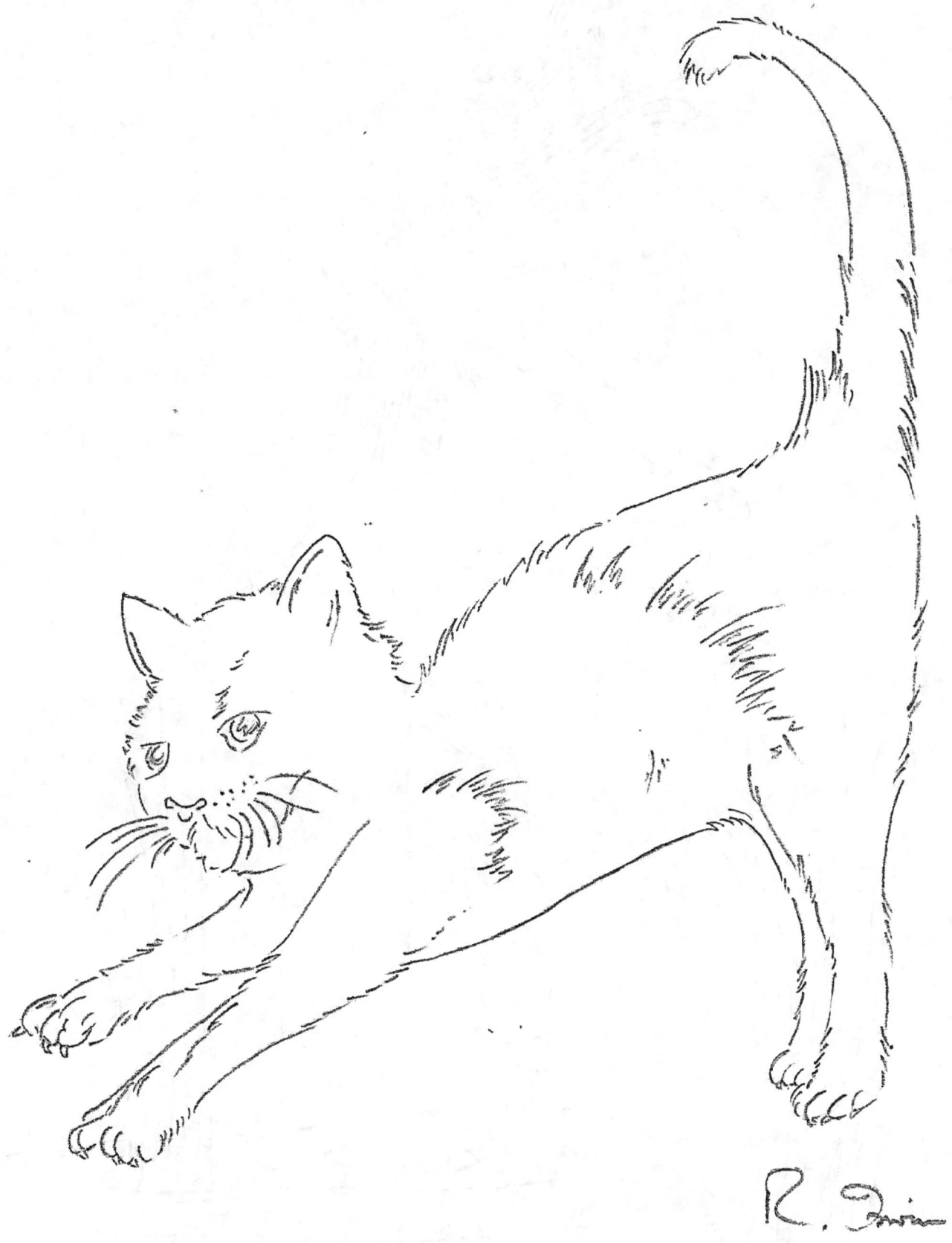

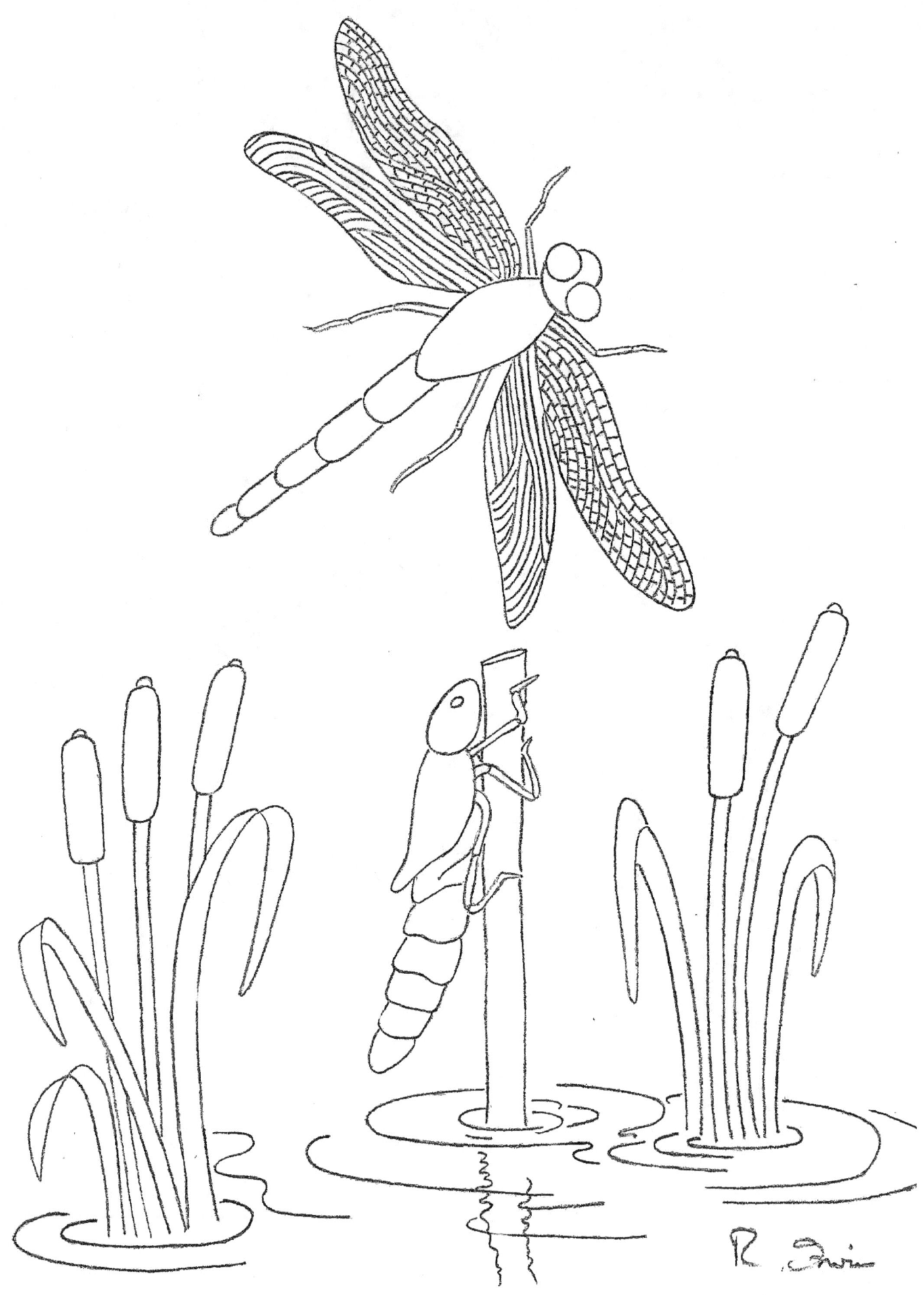

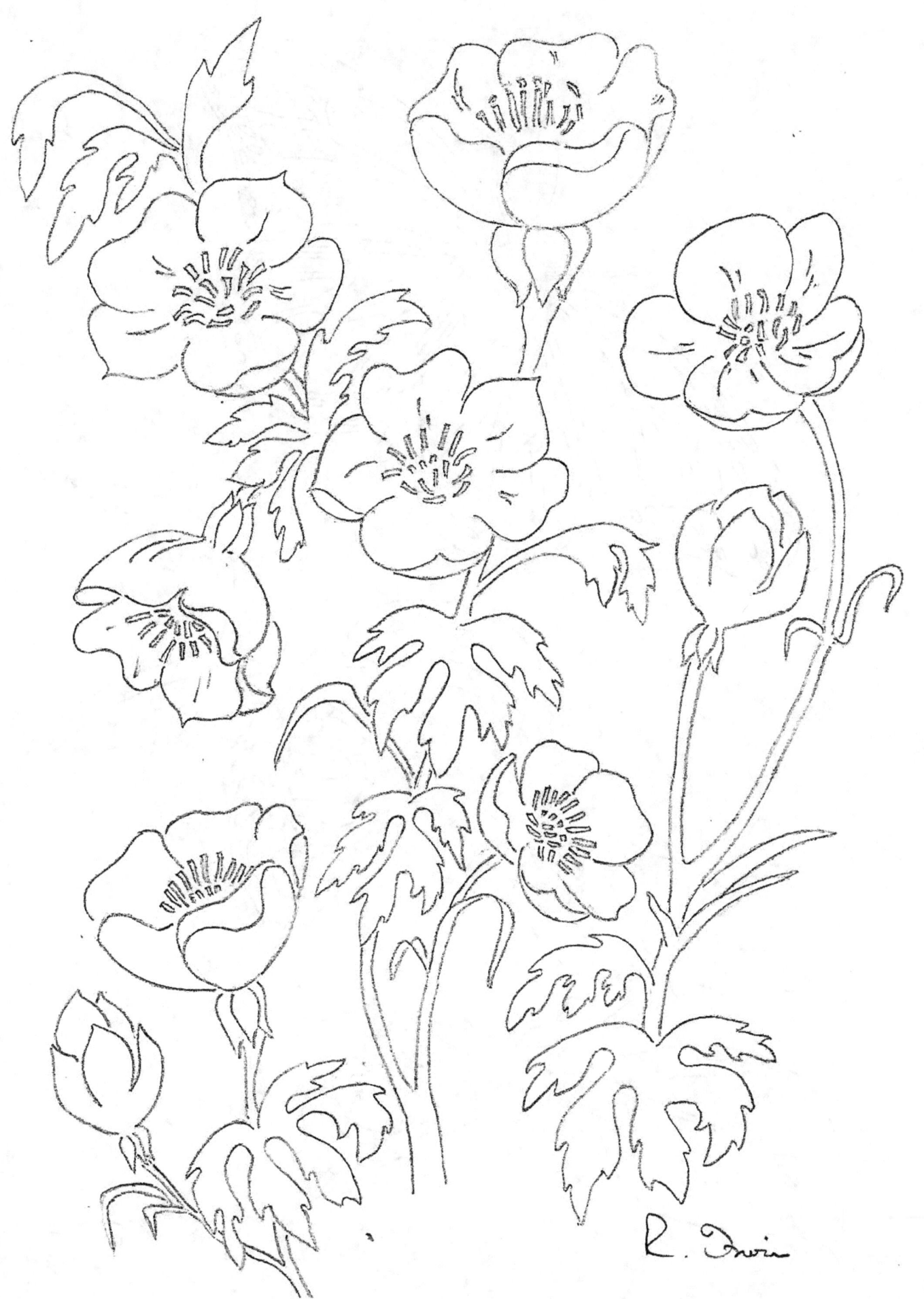

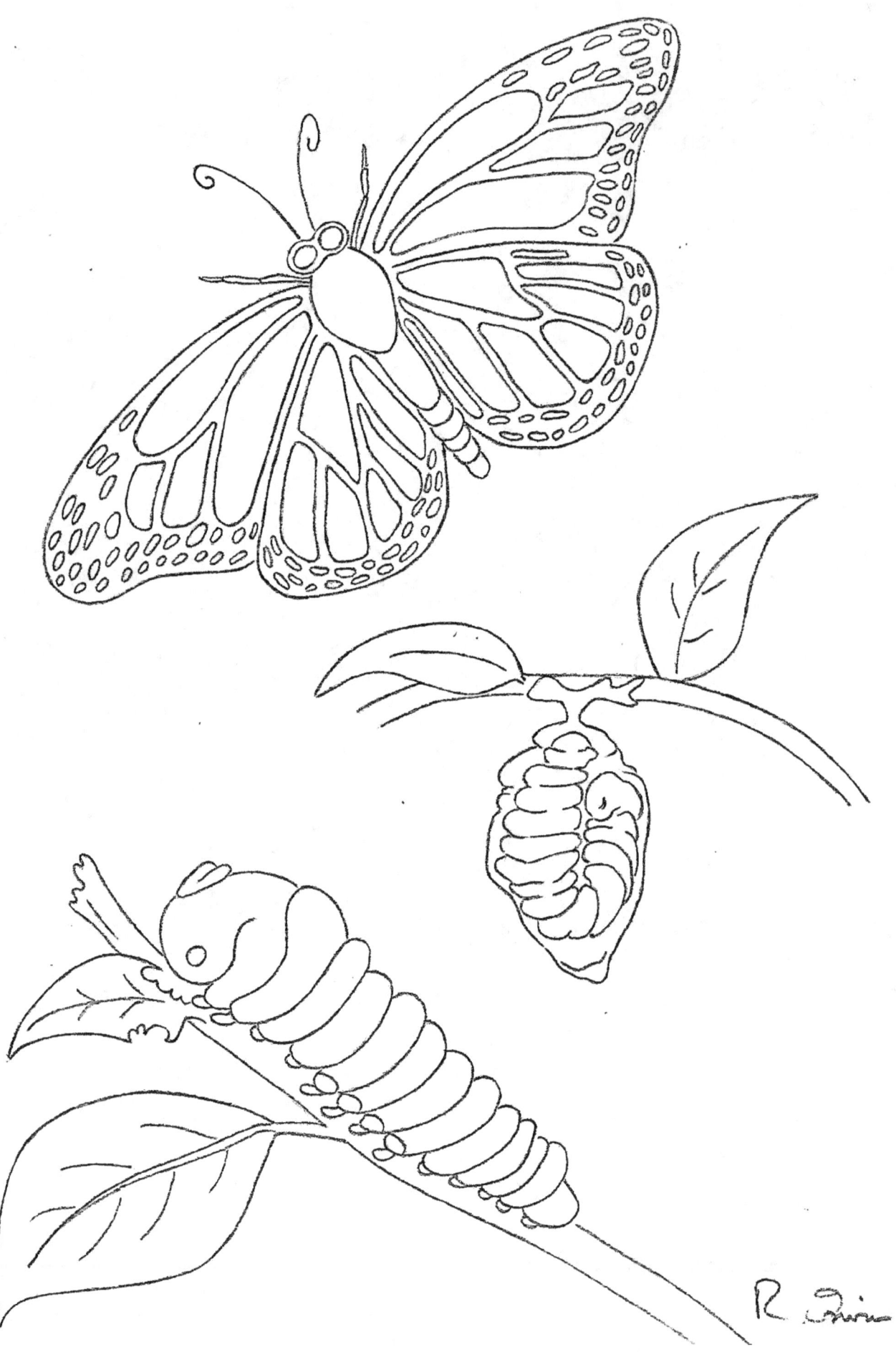

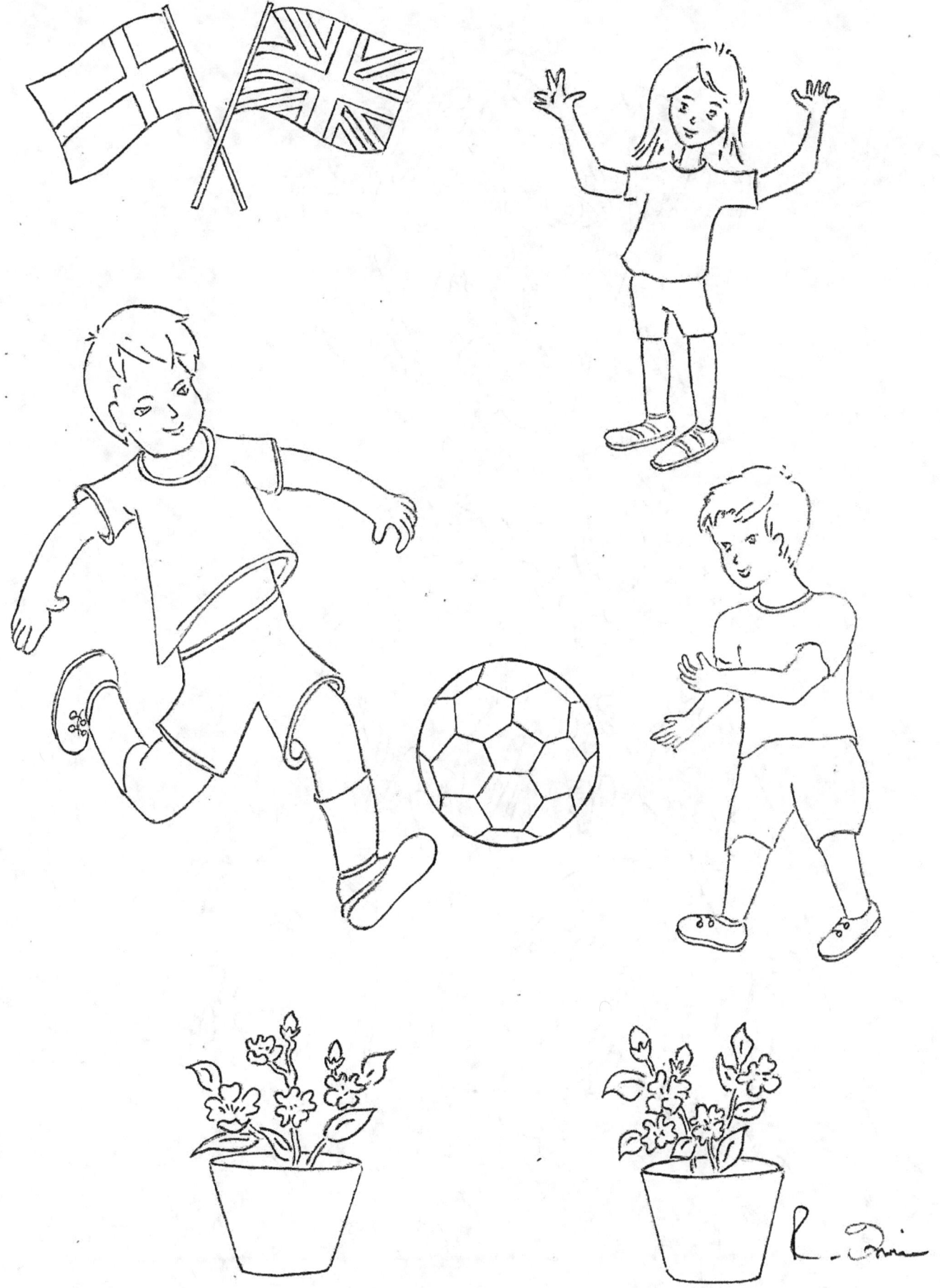

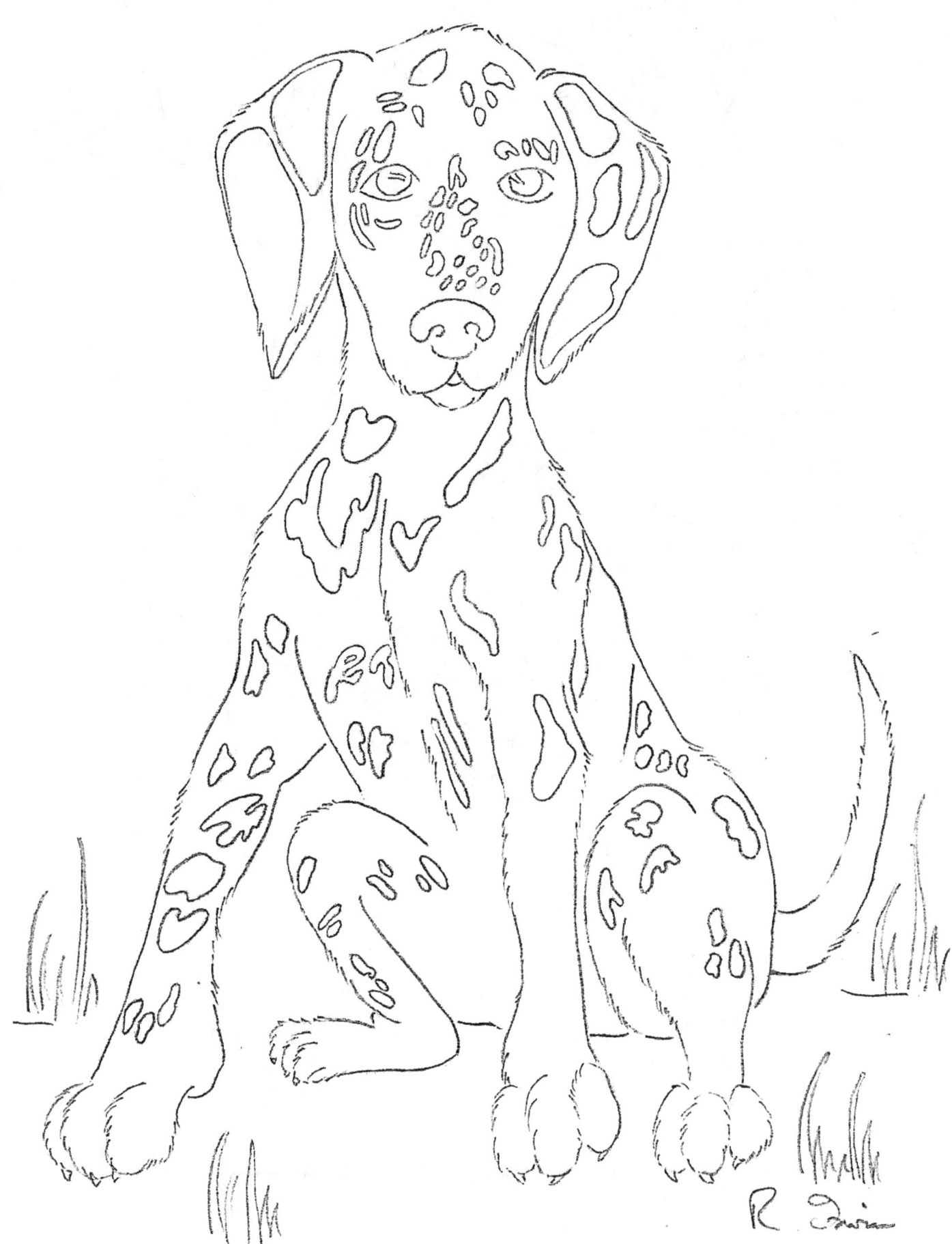

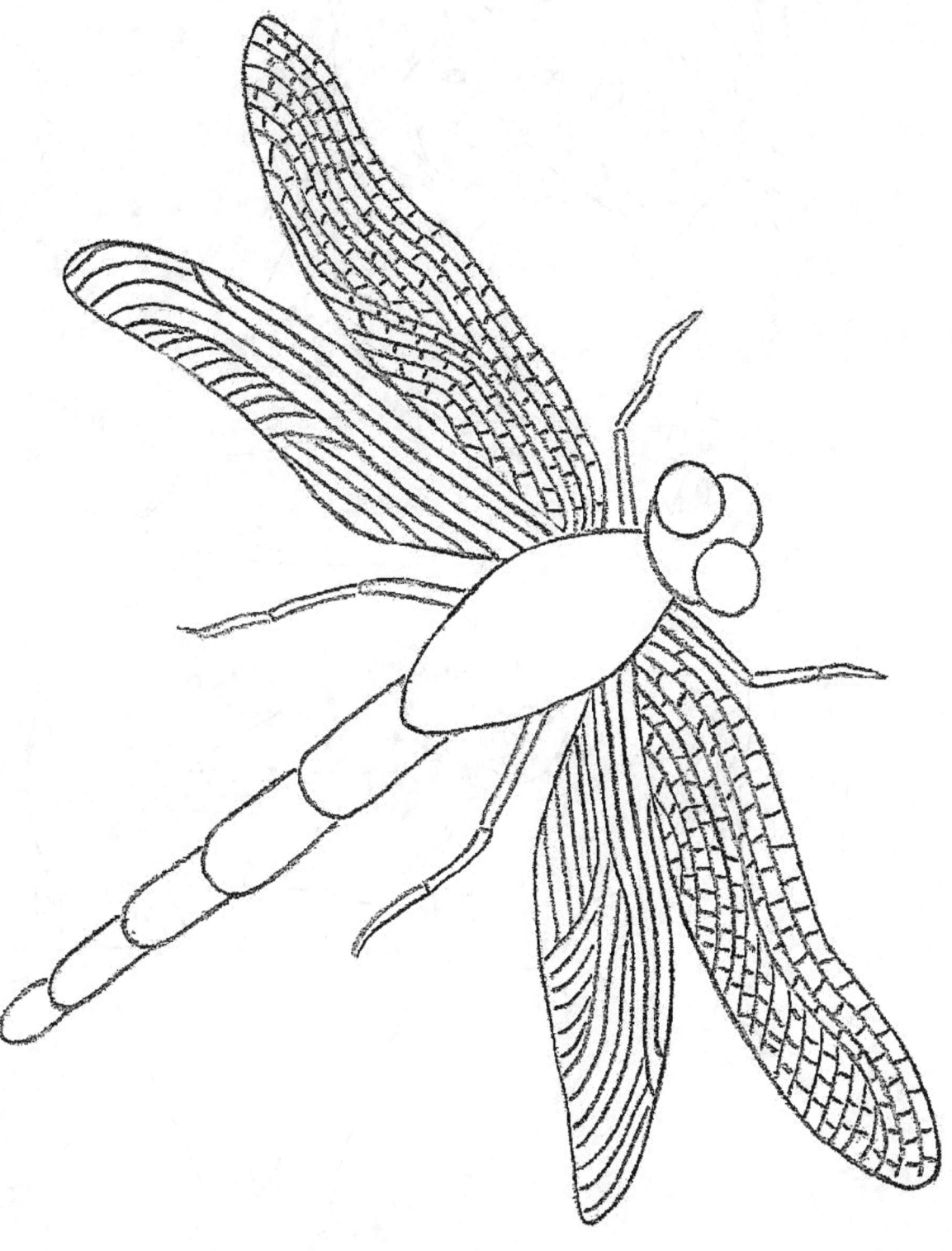

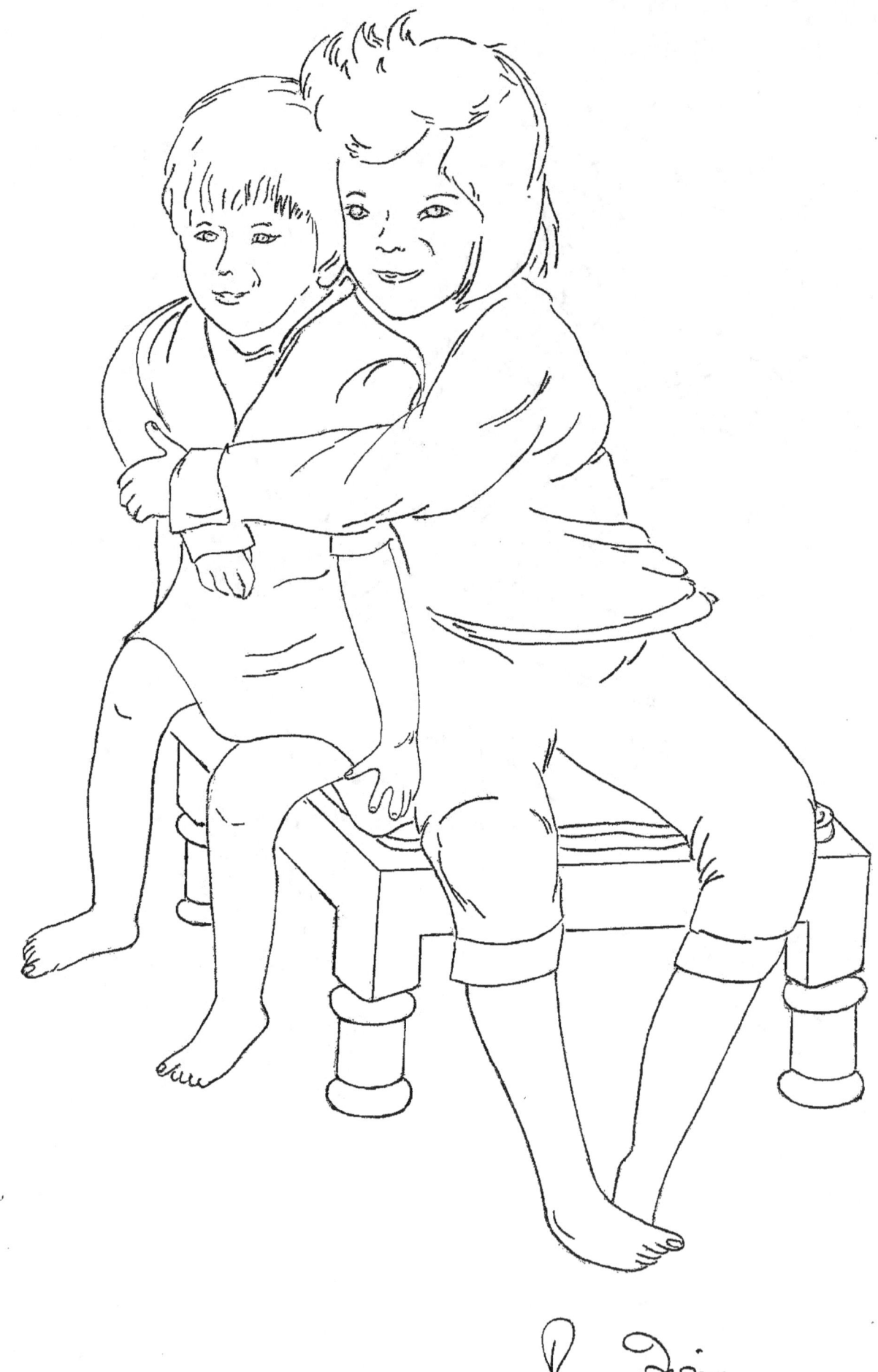

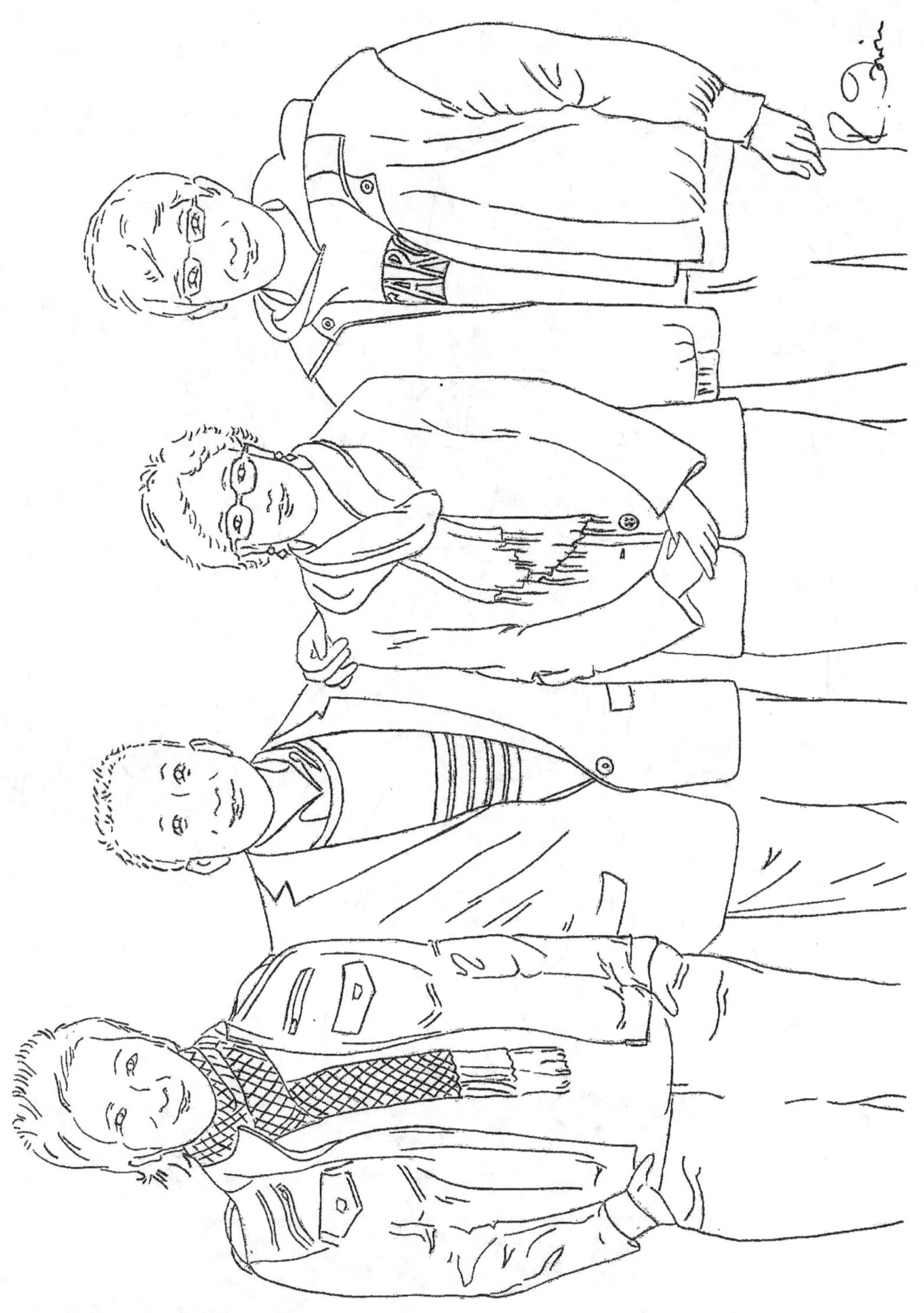

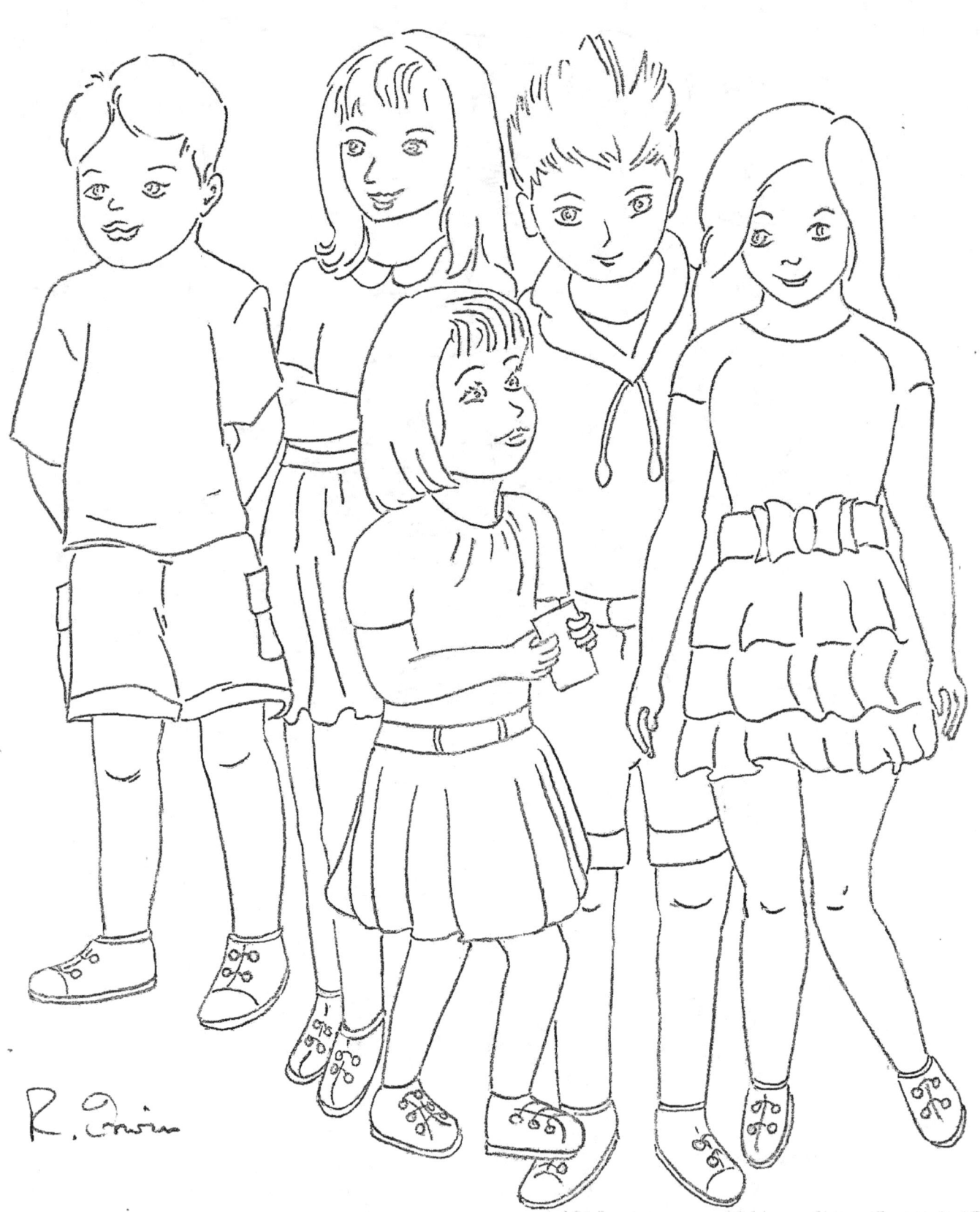

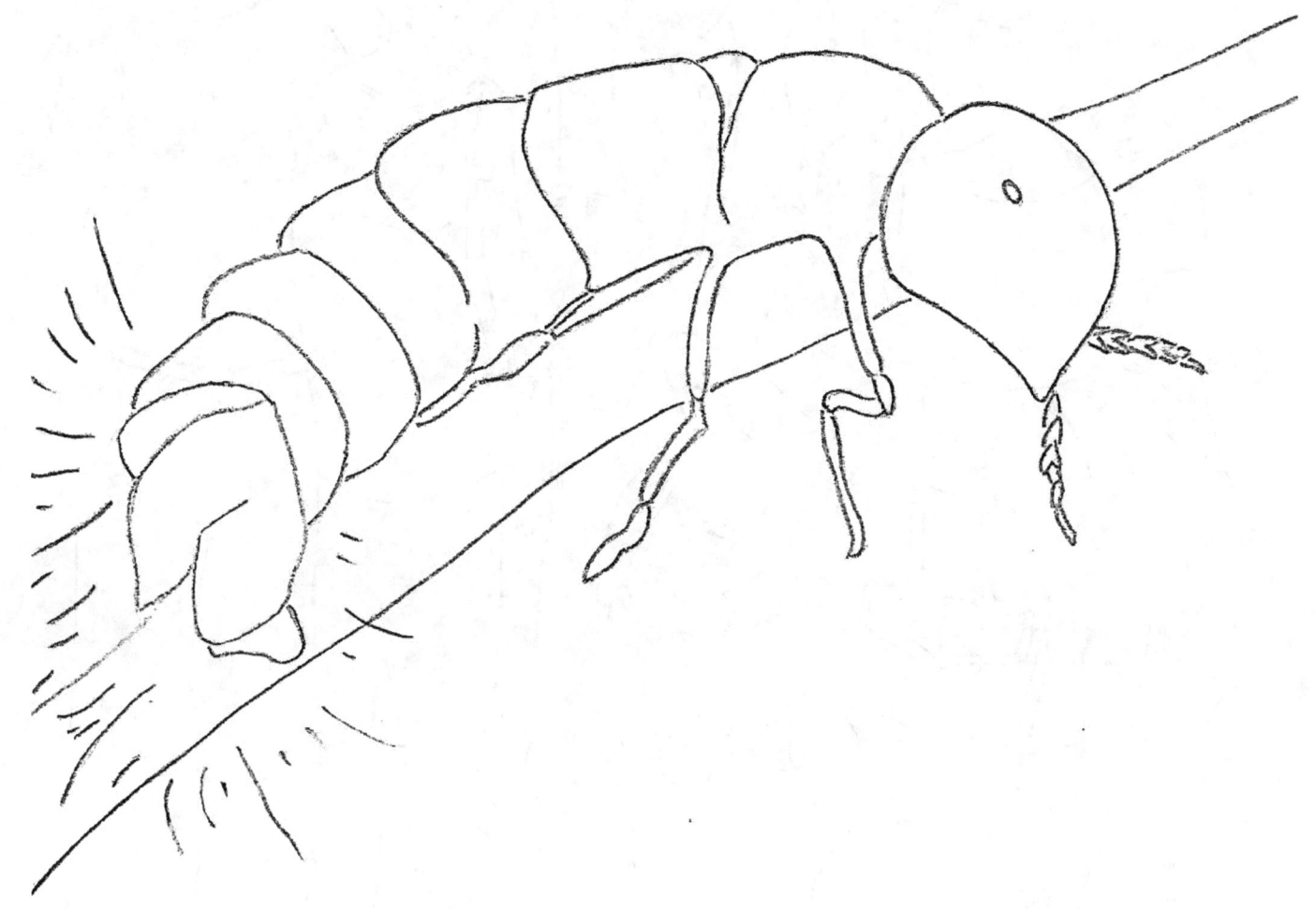

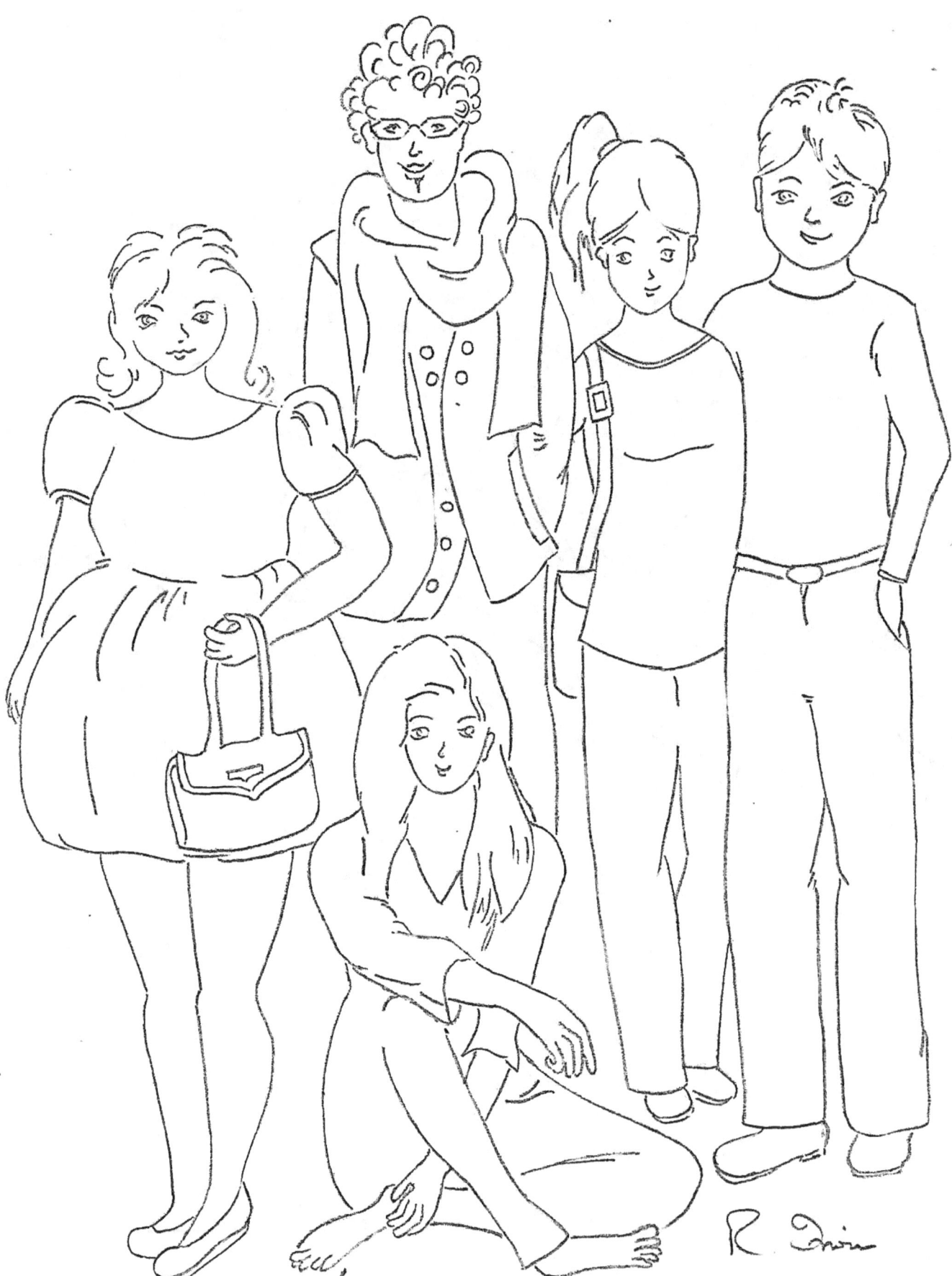

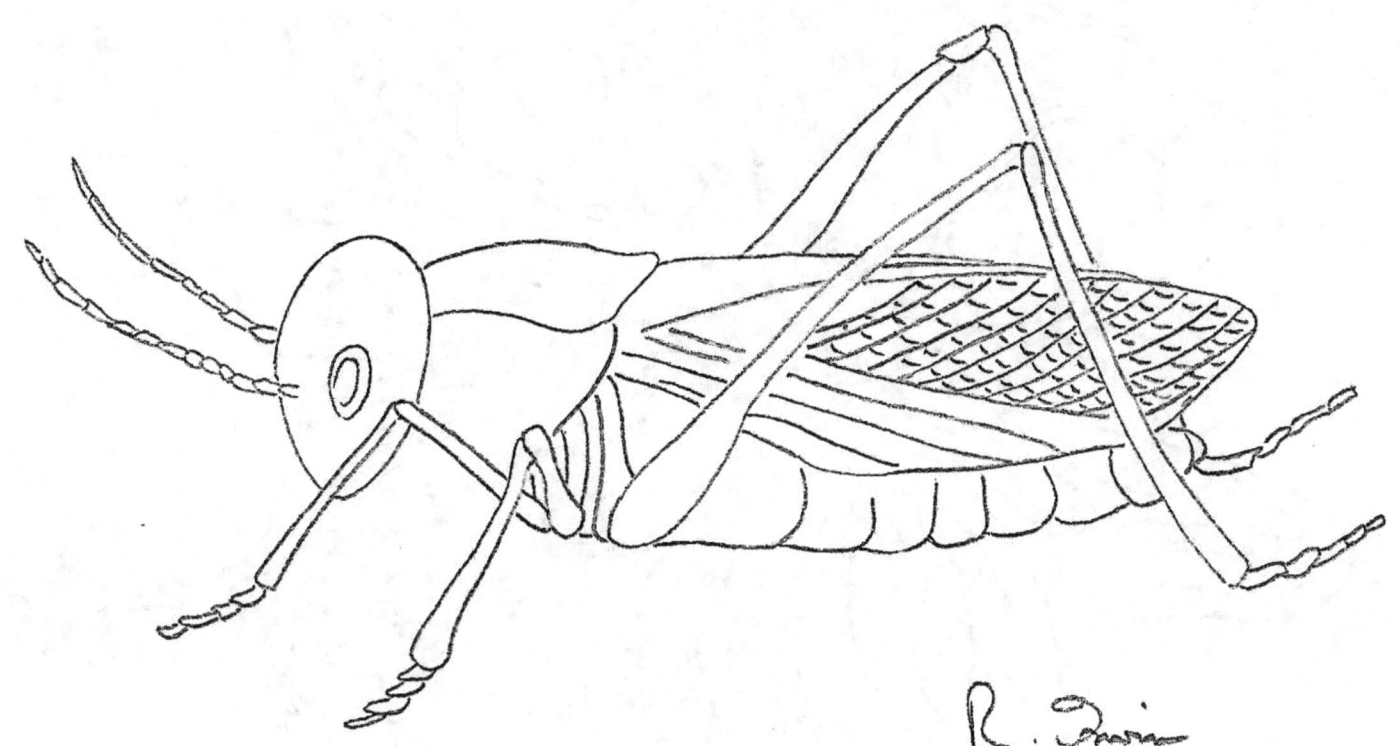

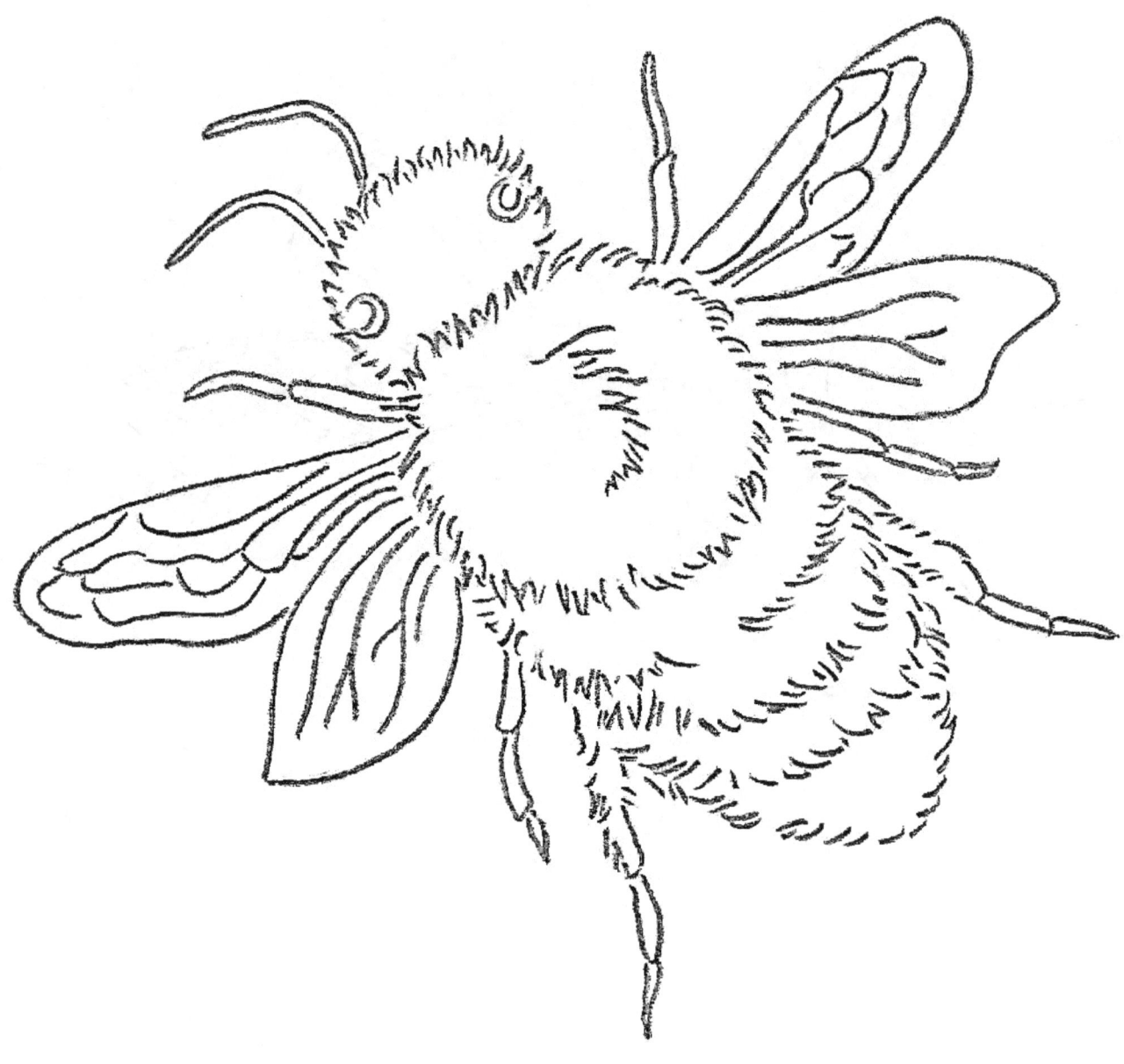

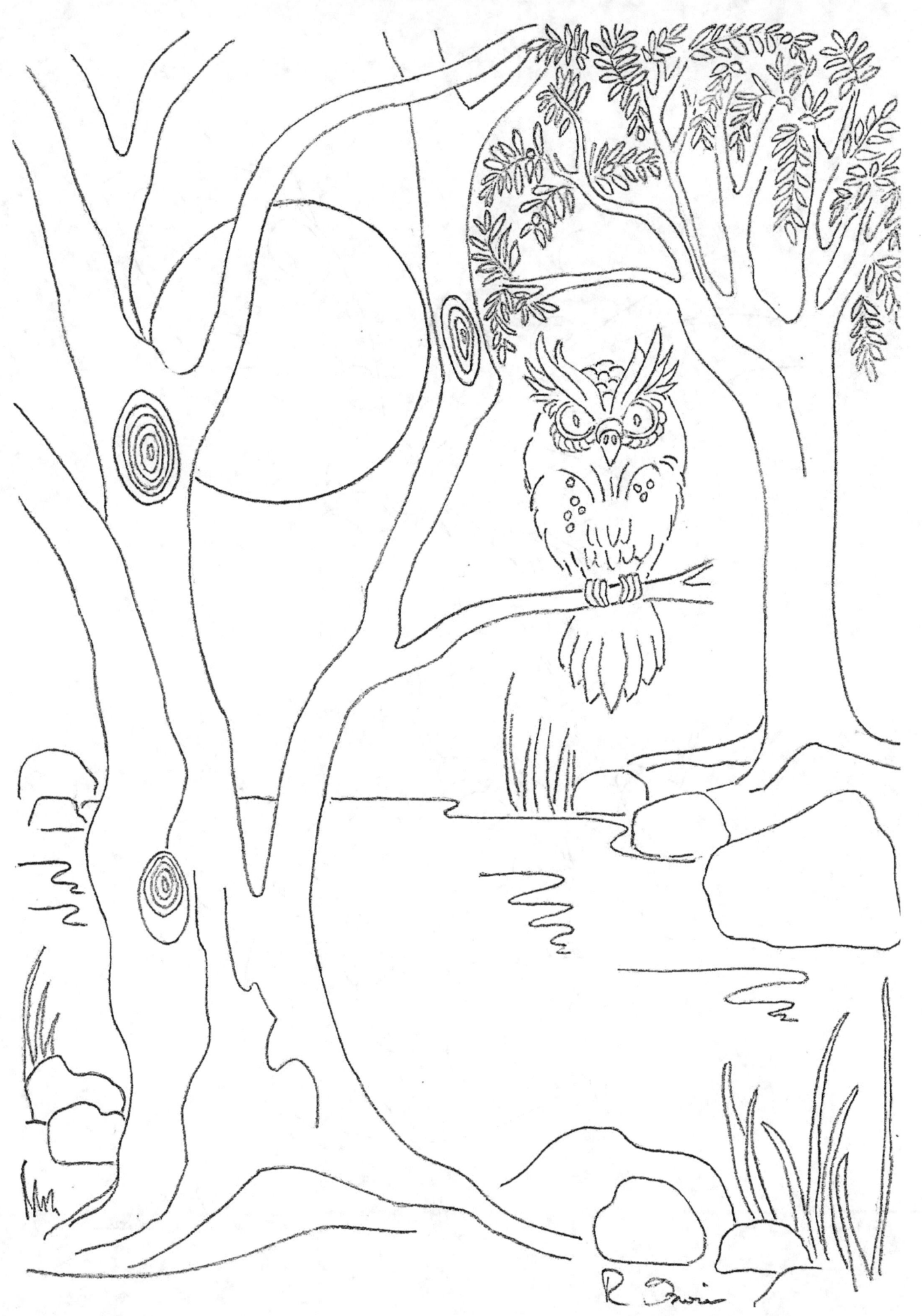

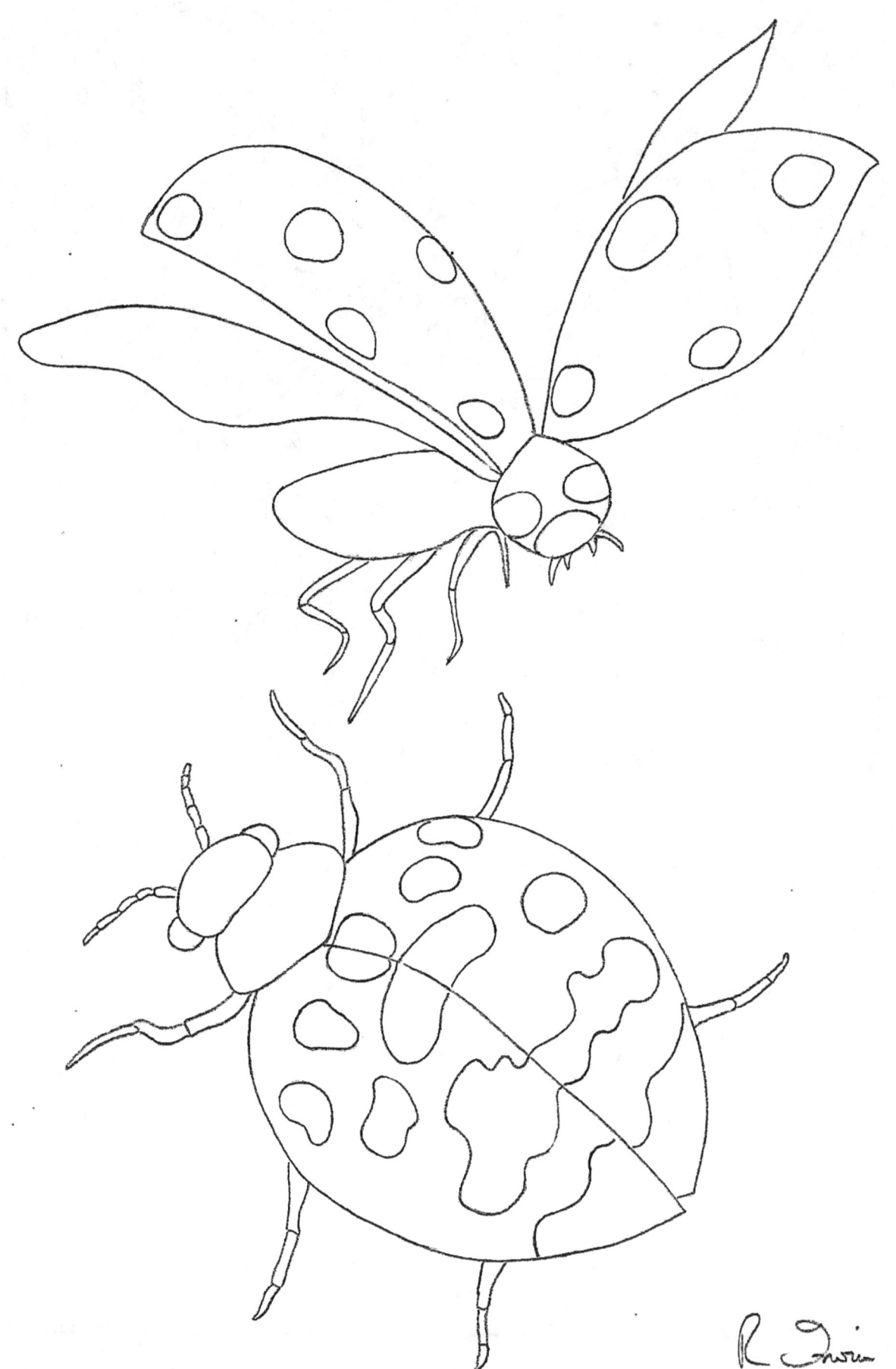

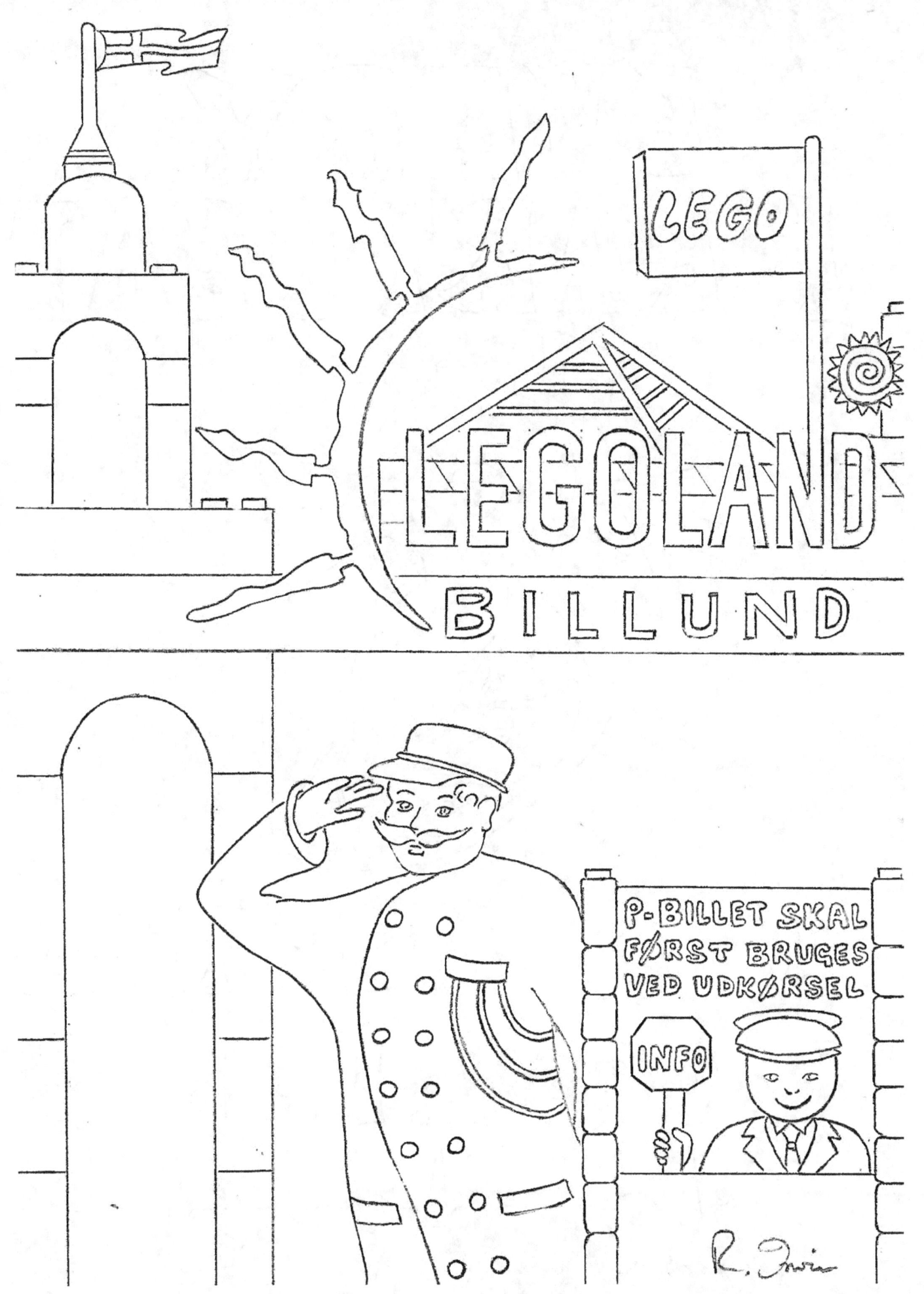

EVERY HEARTBEAT IS A MIRACLE OF LIFE

R. Irwin

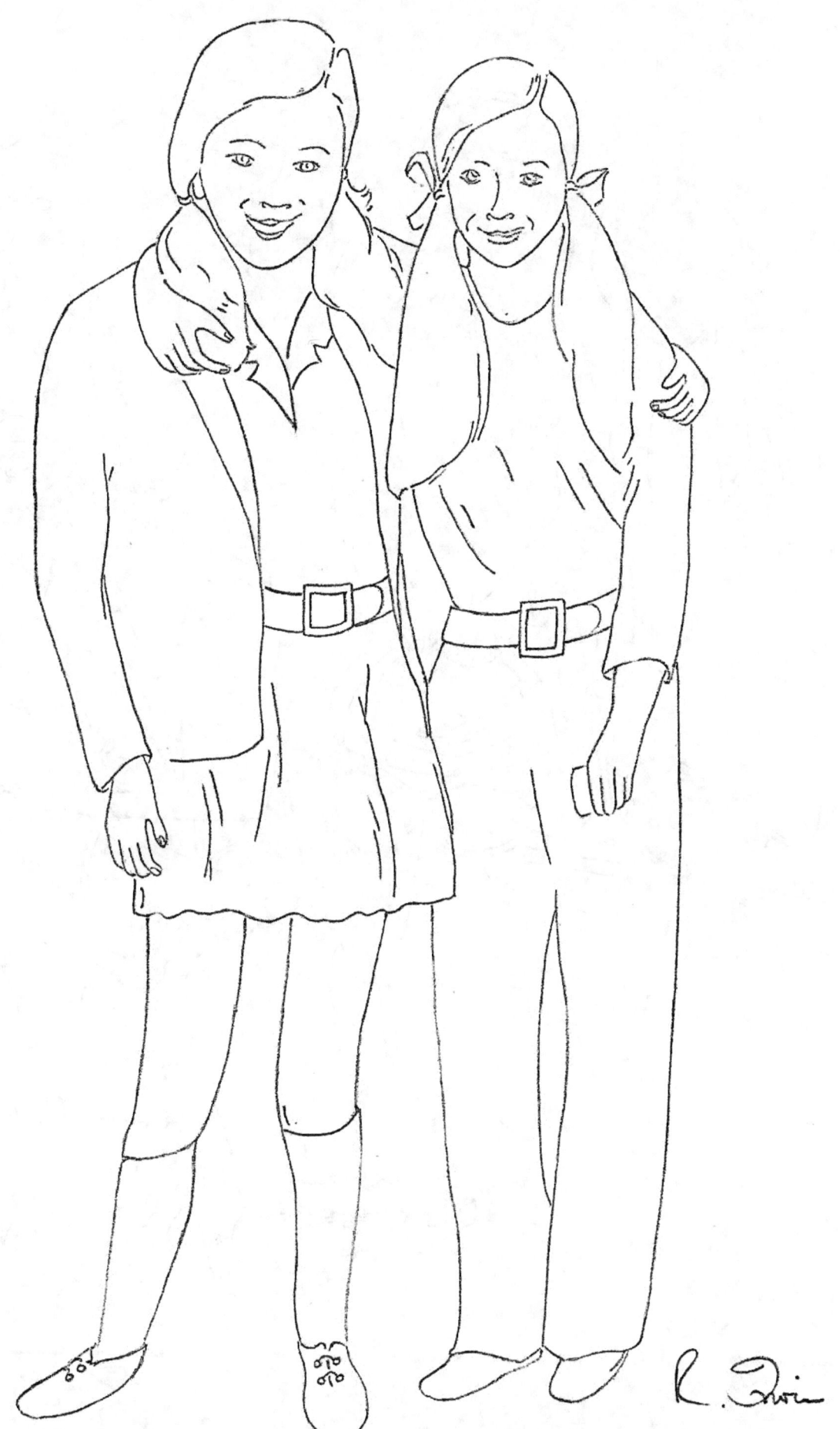

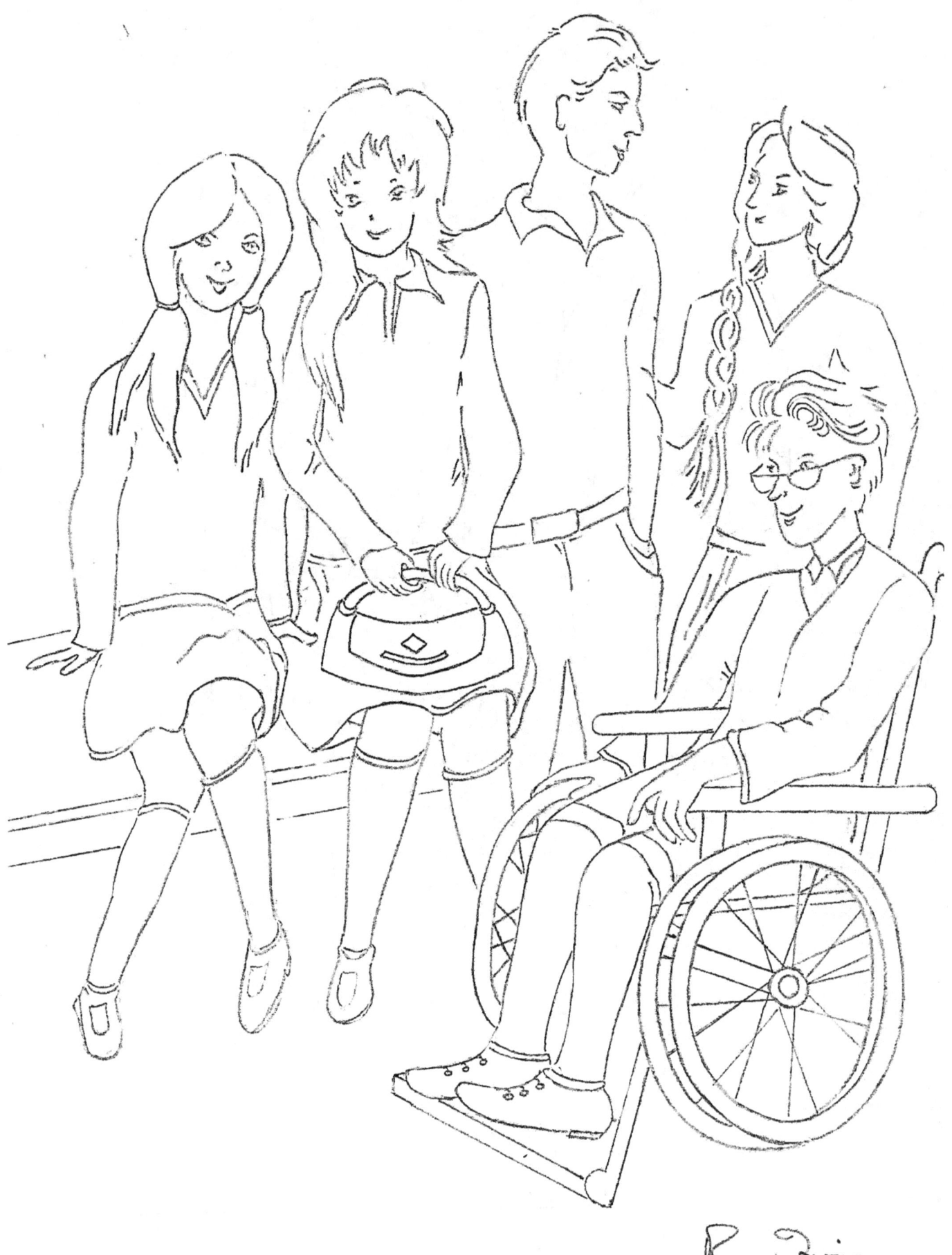

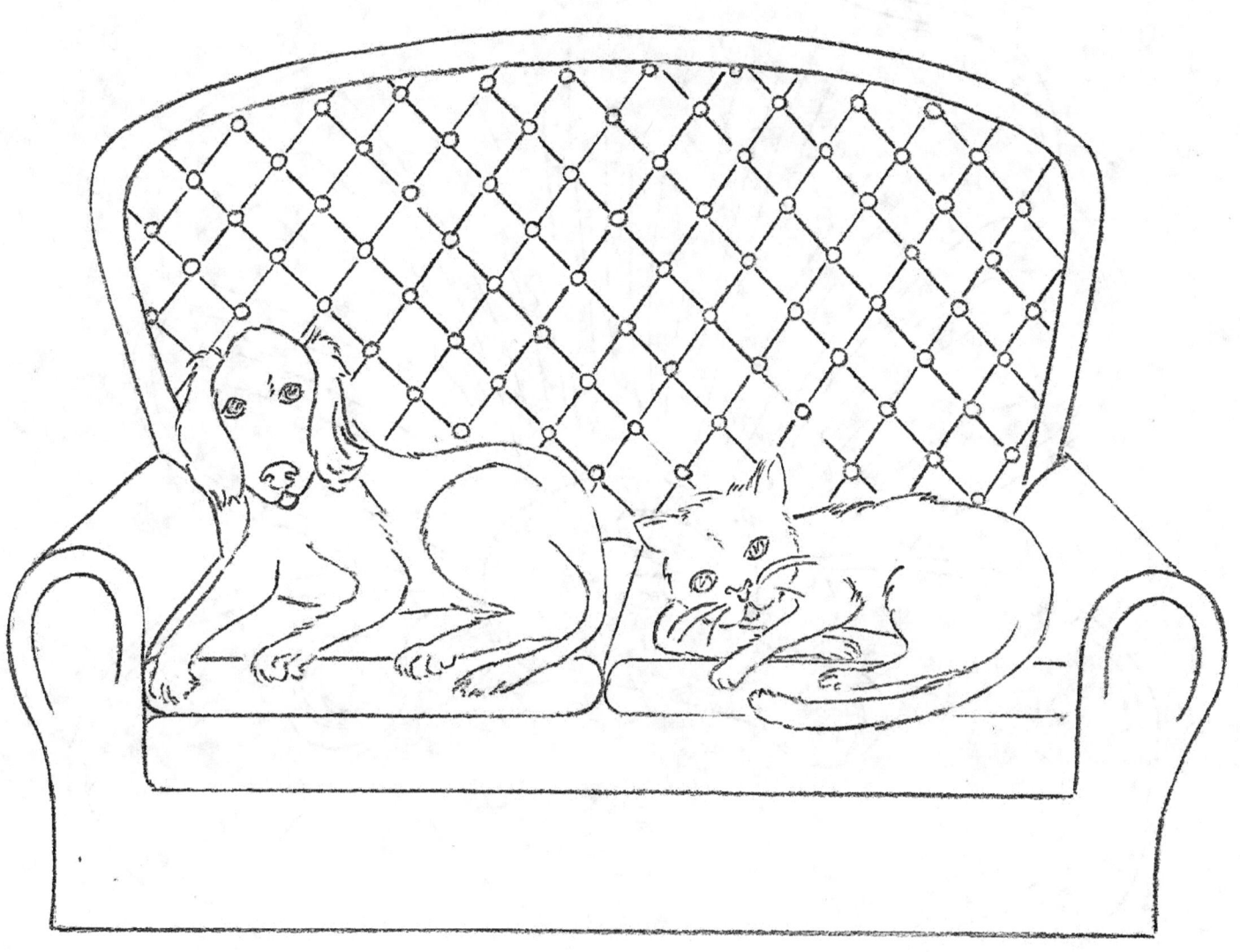

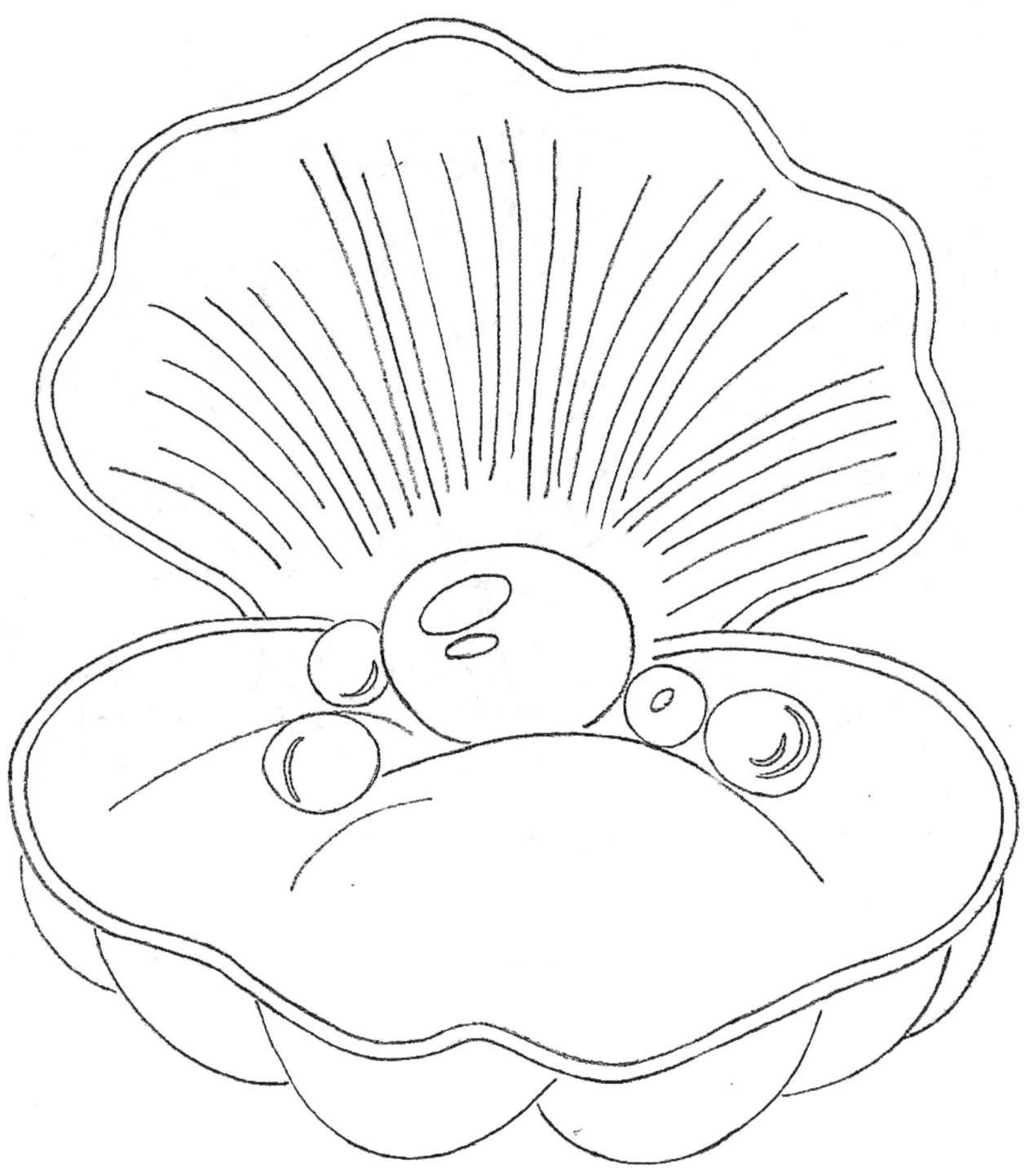

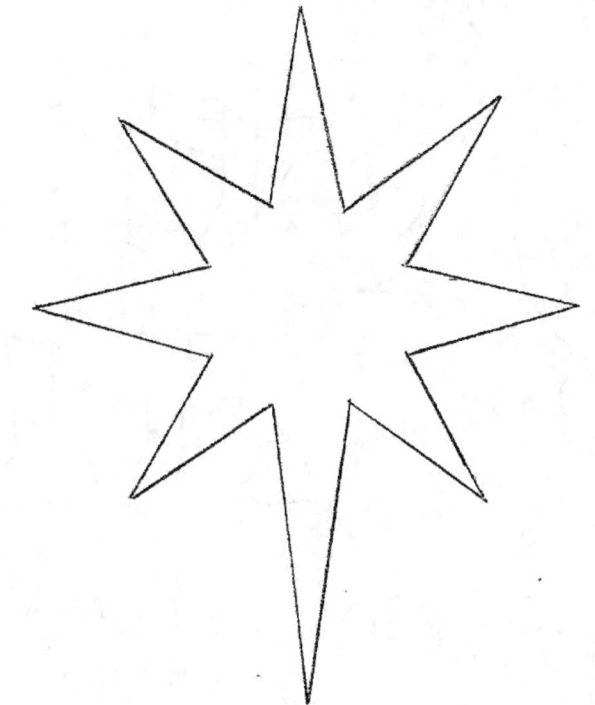
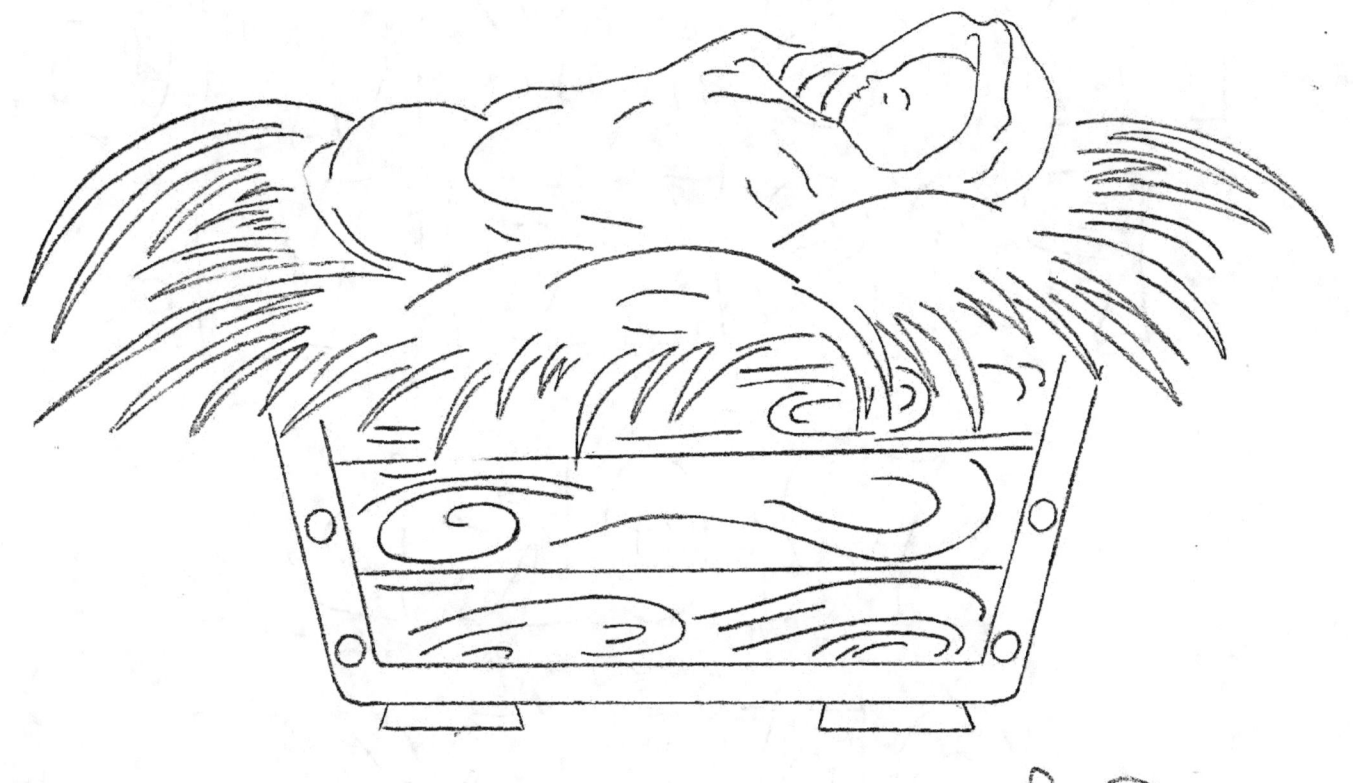

SPEAK YOUR BLESSINGS INTO EXISTENCE; BY SAYING POSITIVE WORDS ONLY!

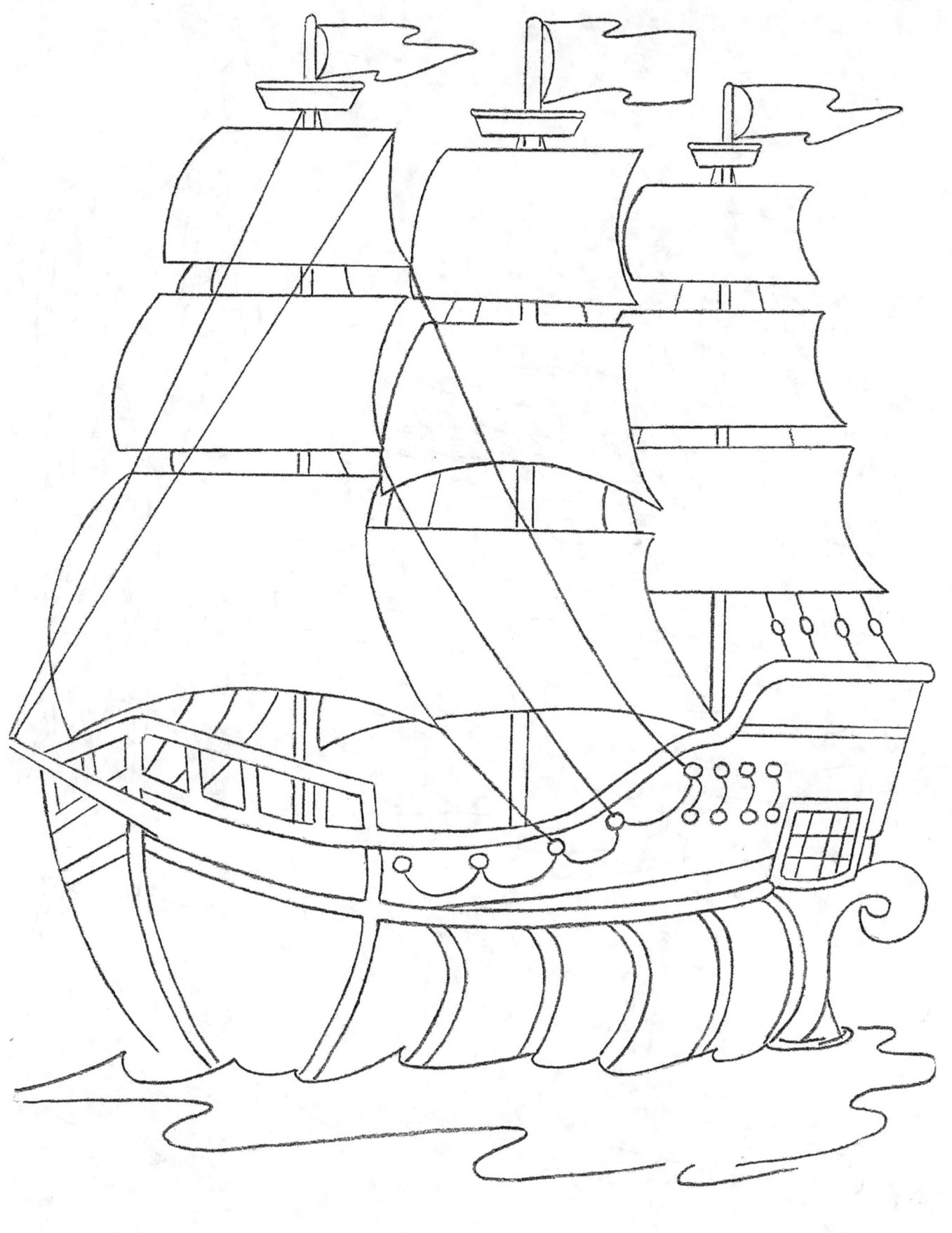

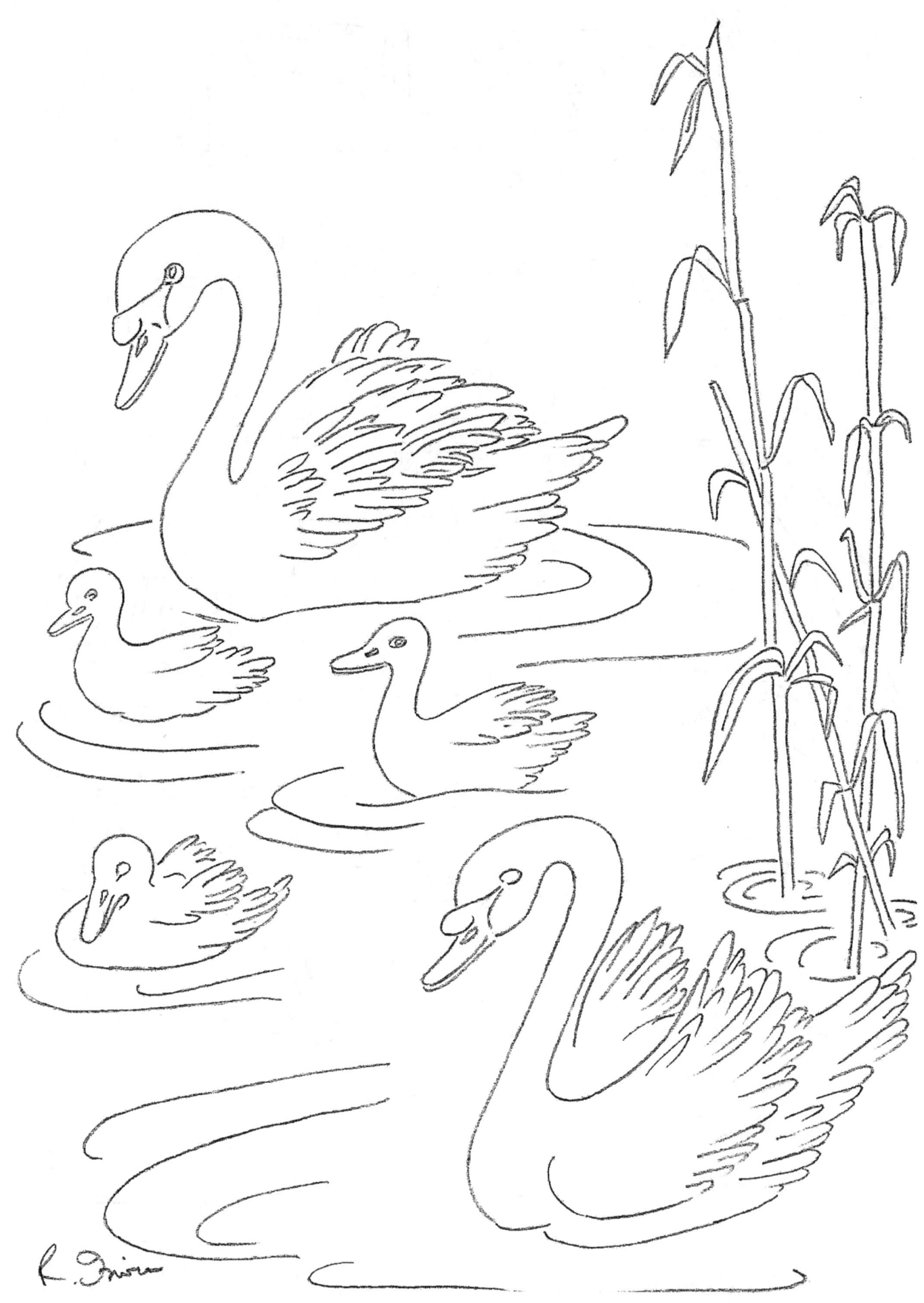

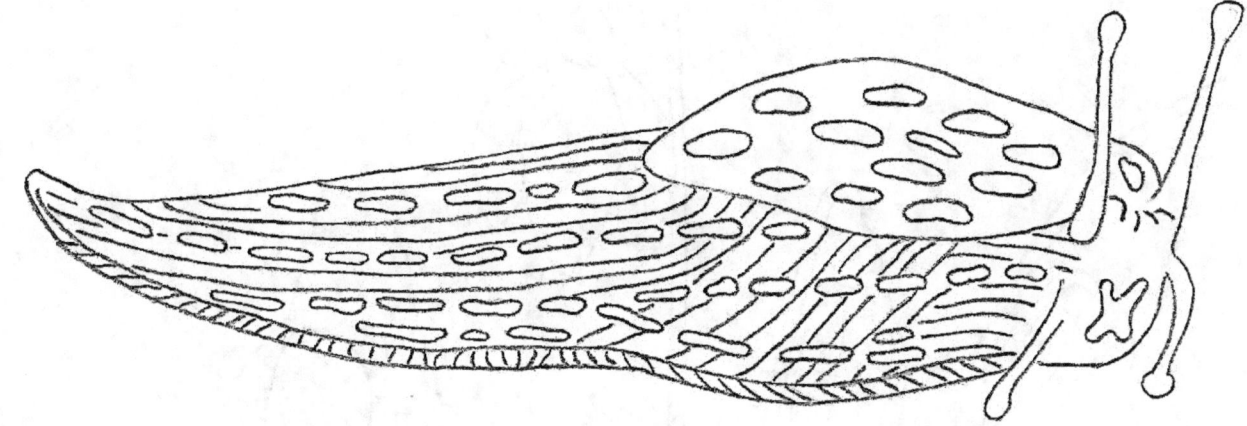

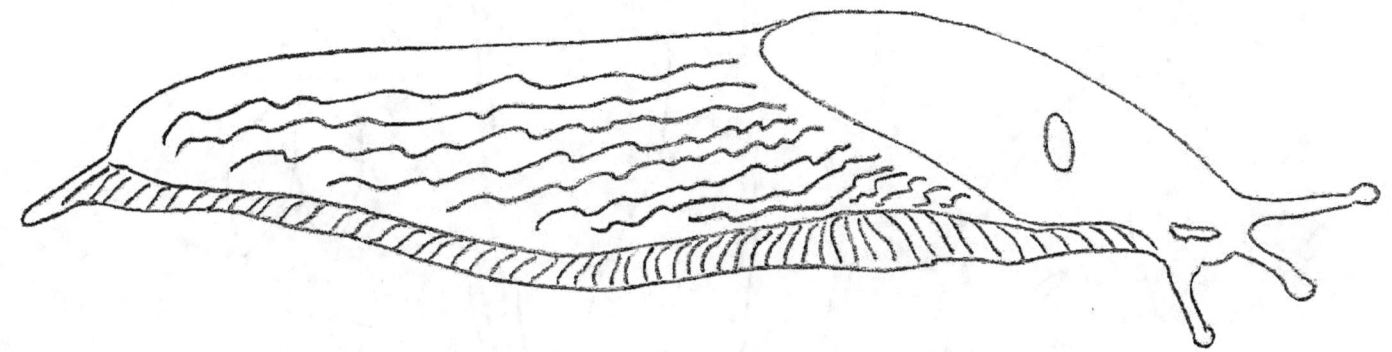

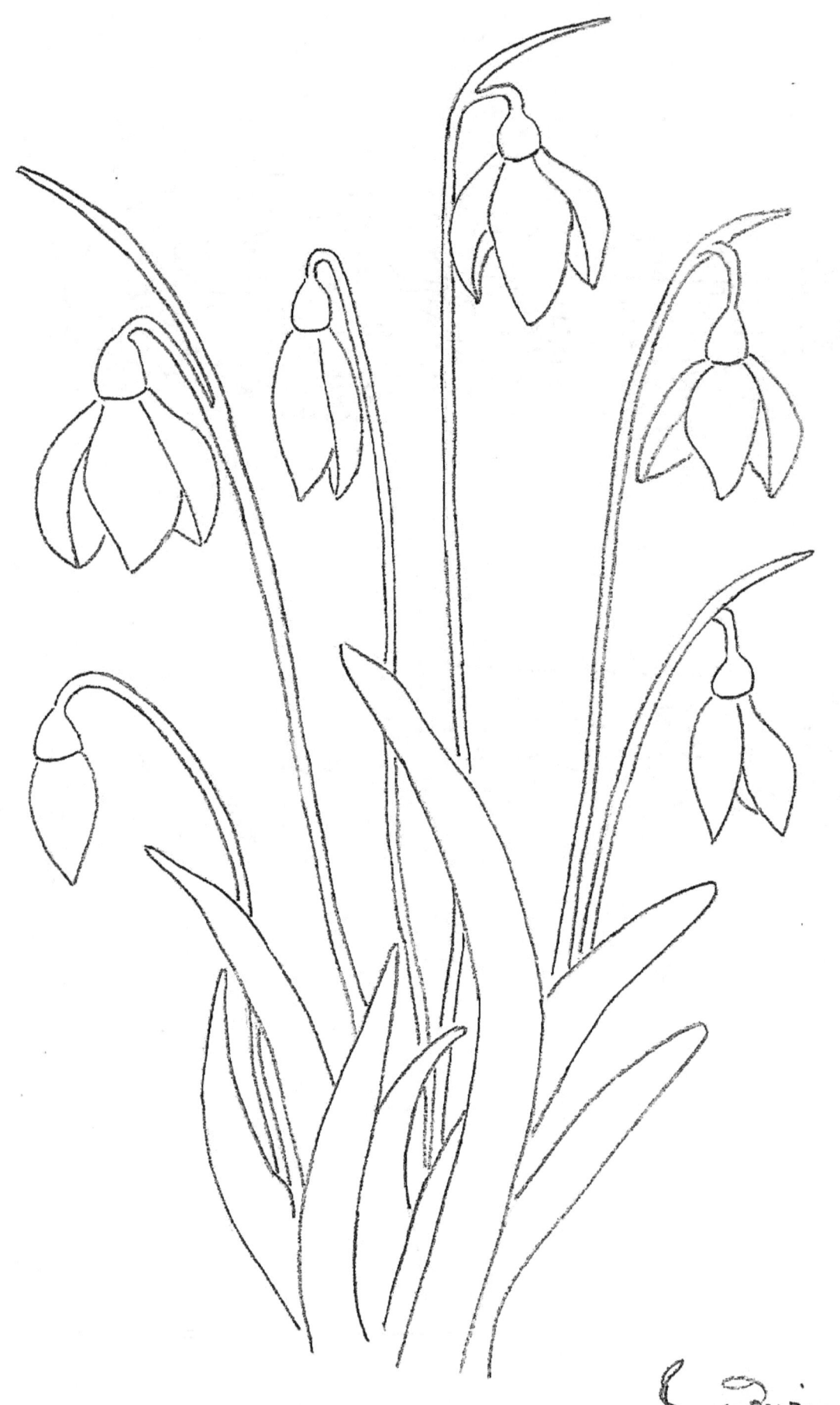

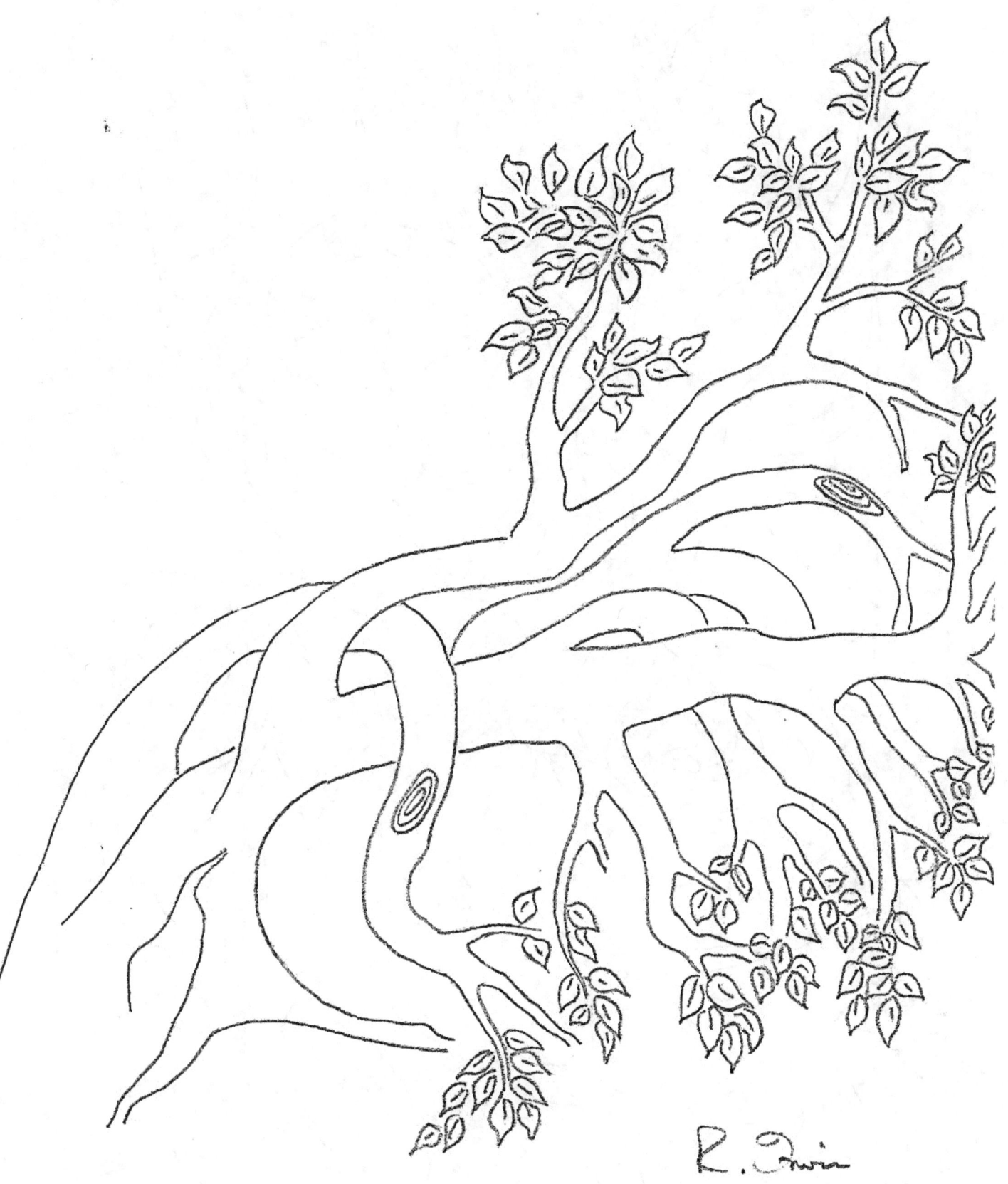

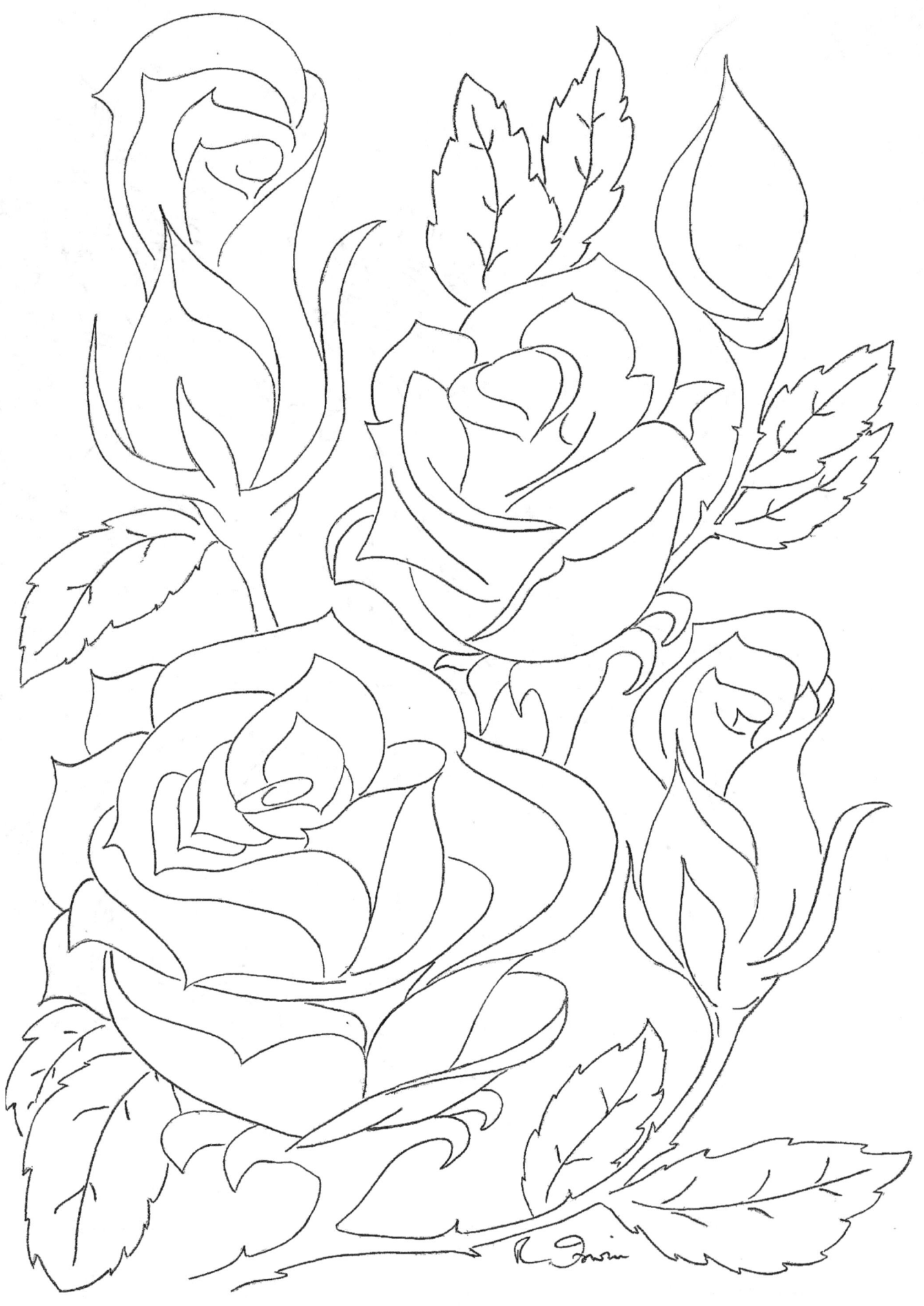

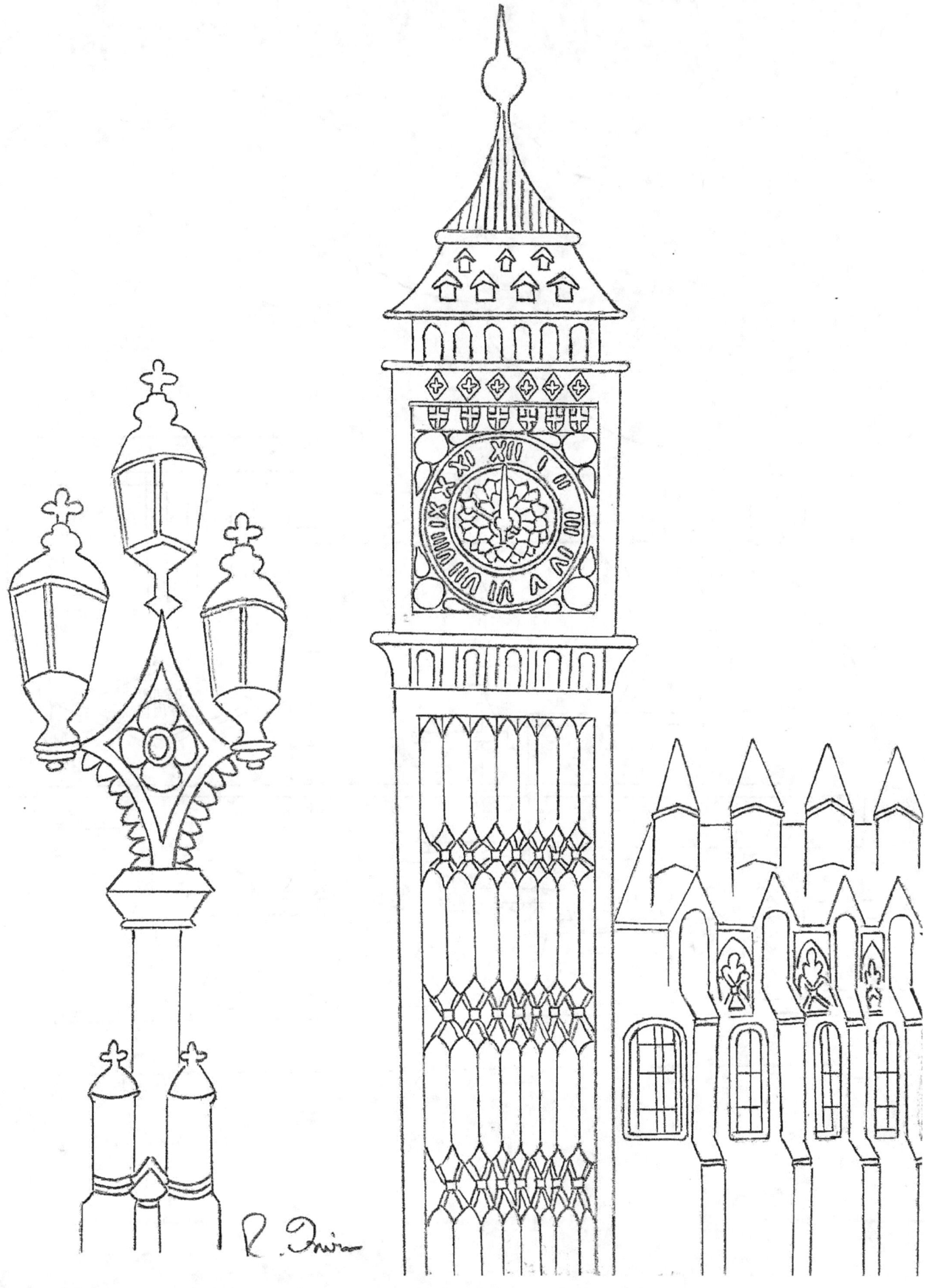

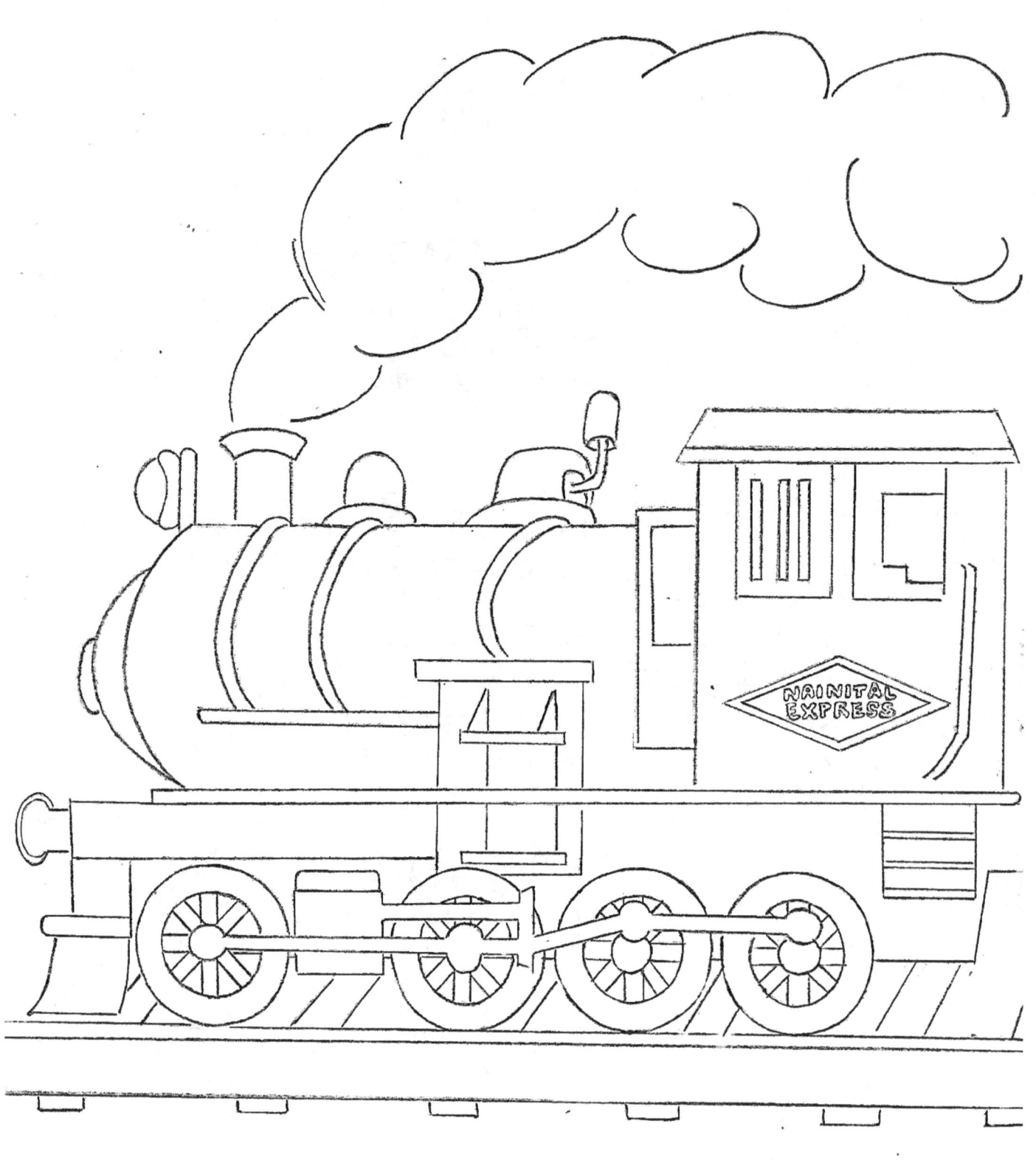

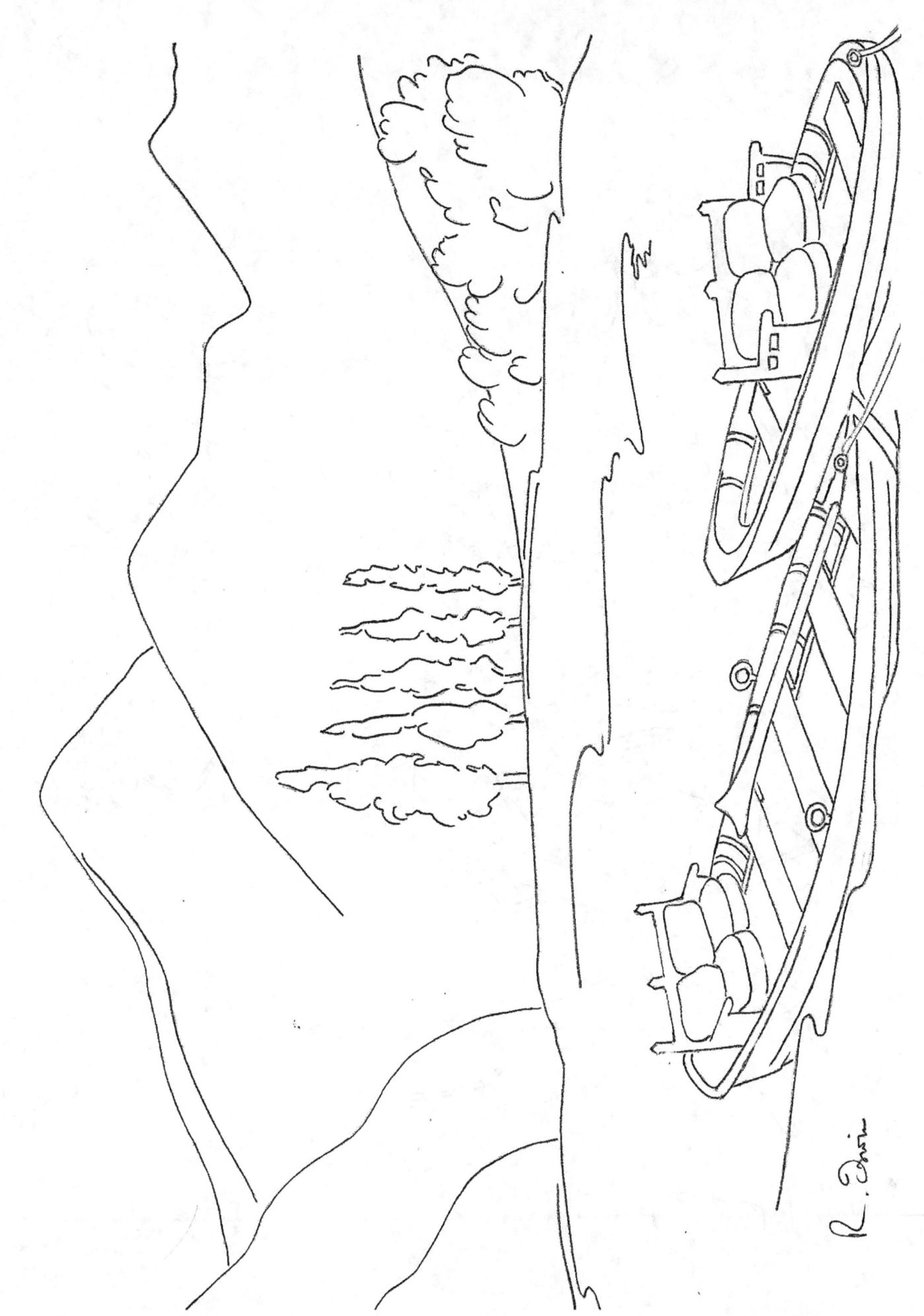

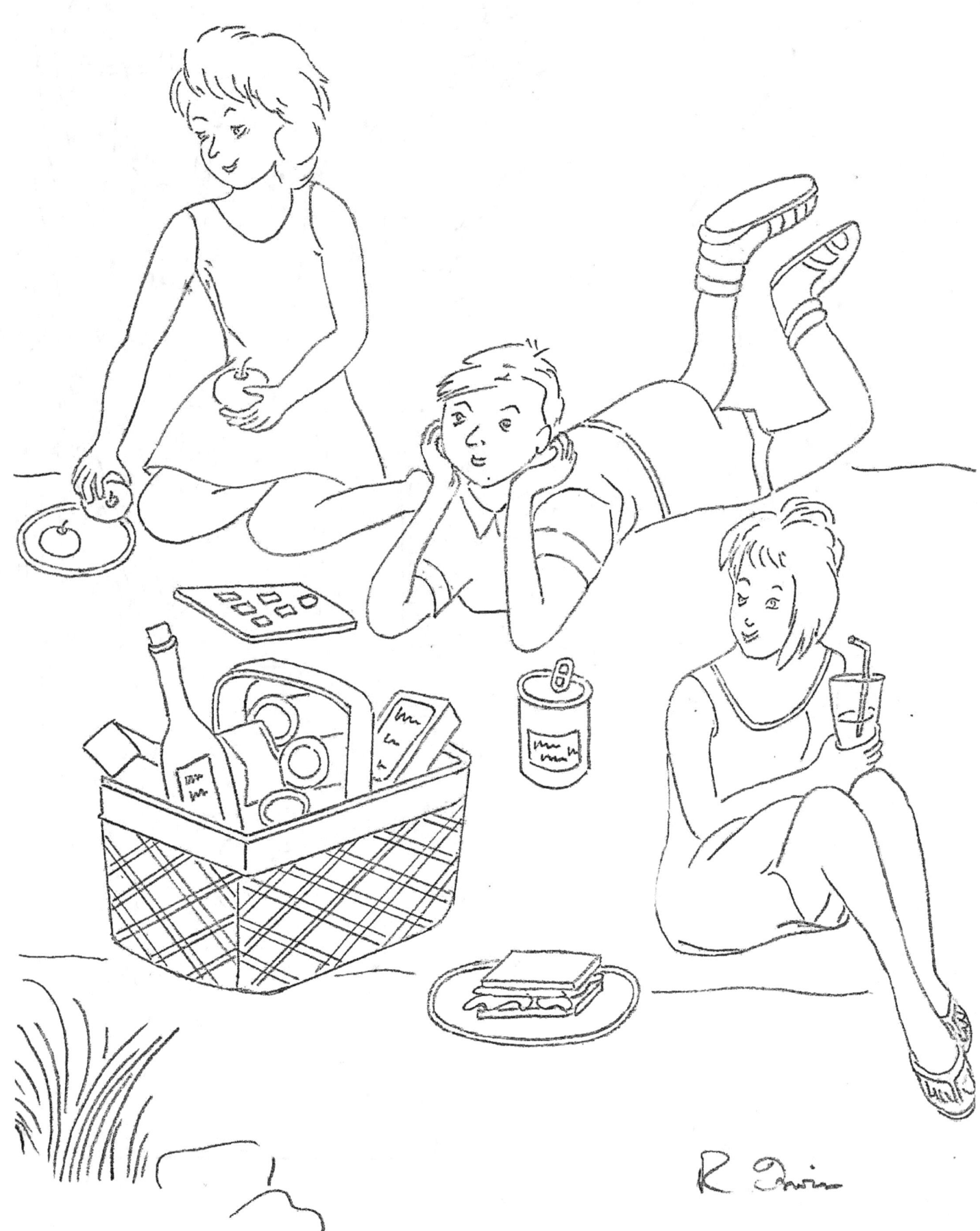

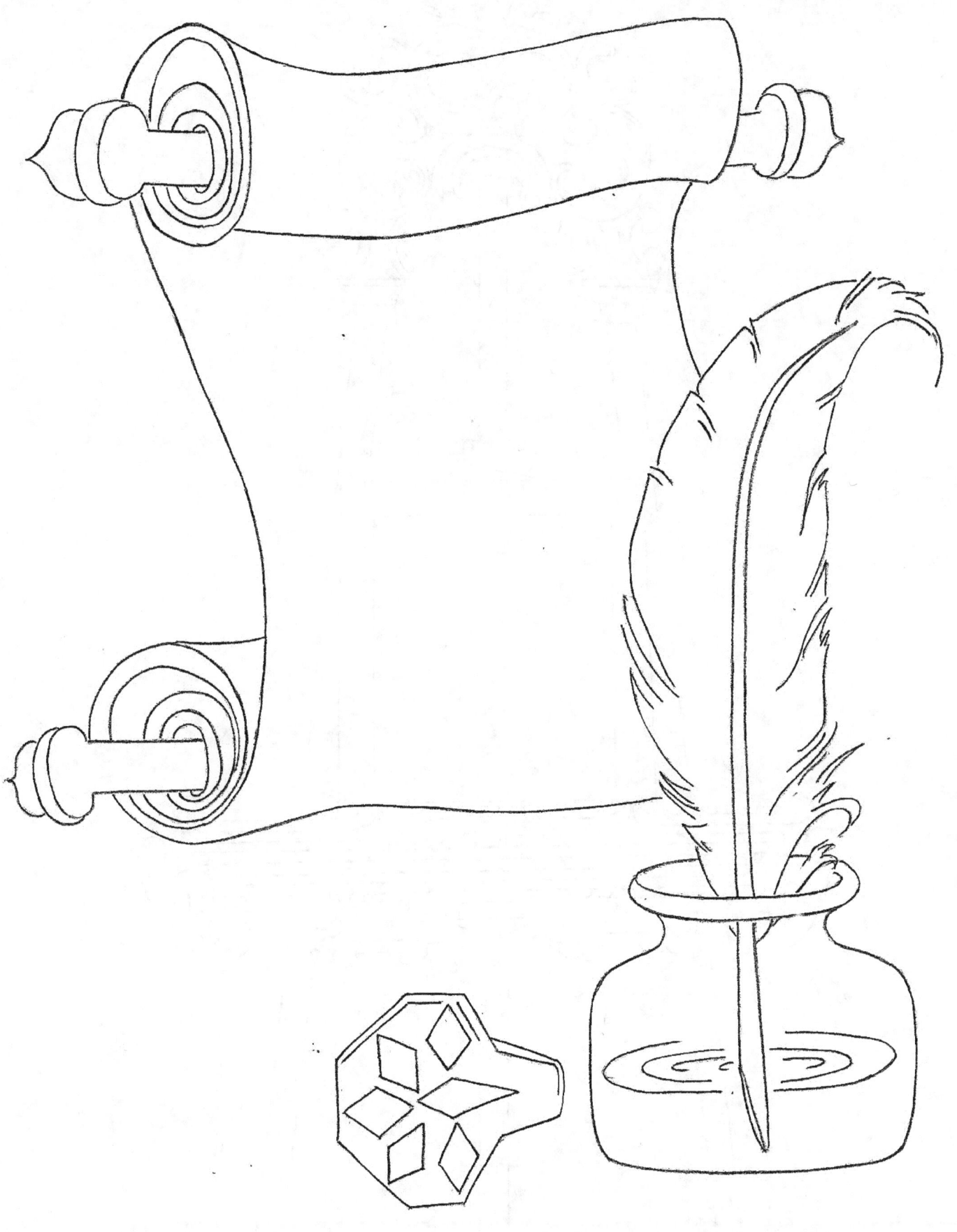

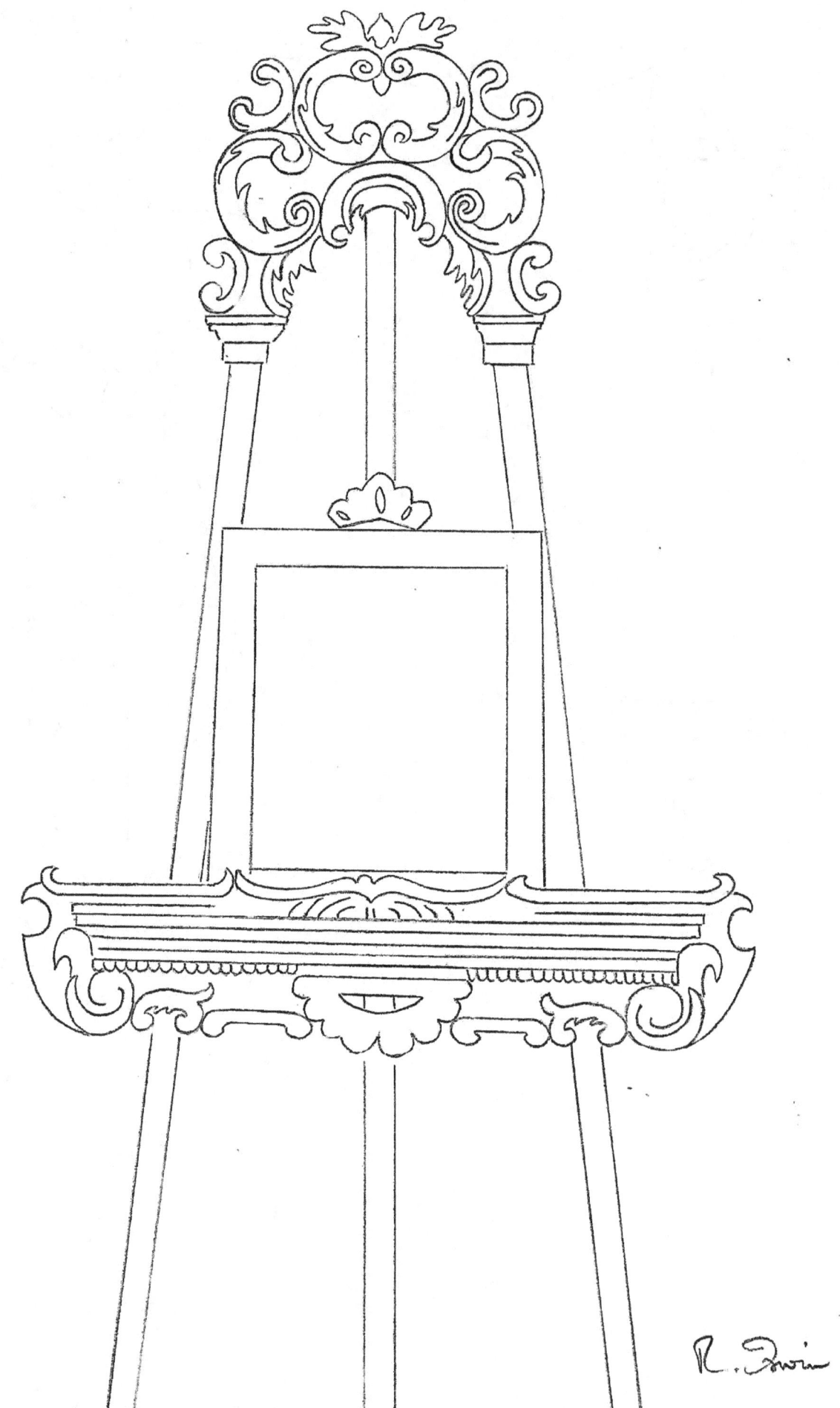

JOIN THE DOTS

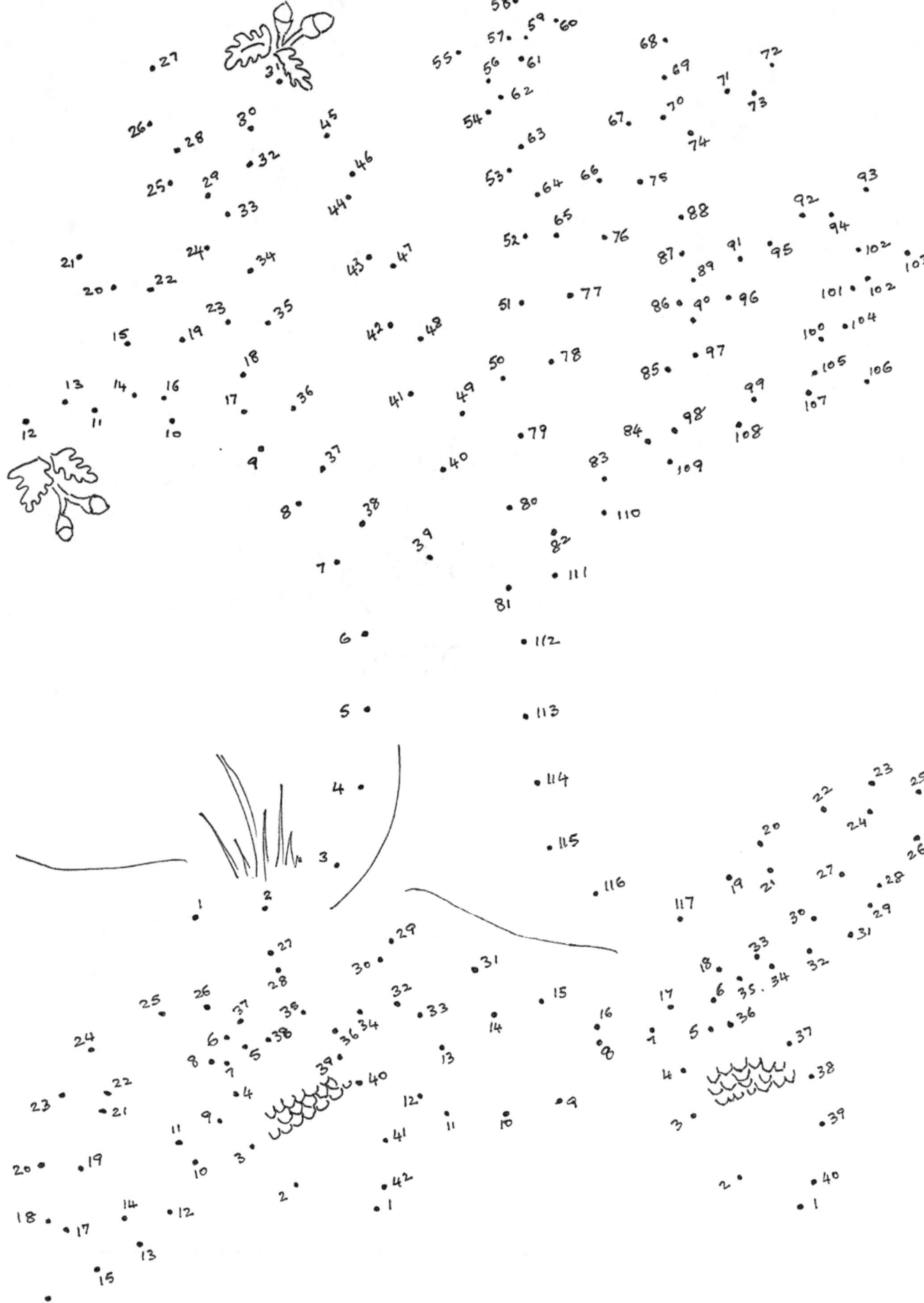

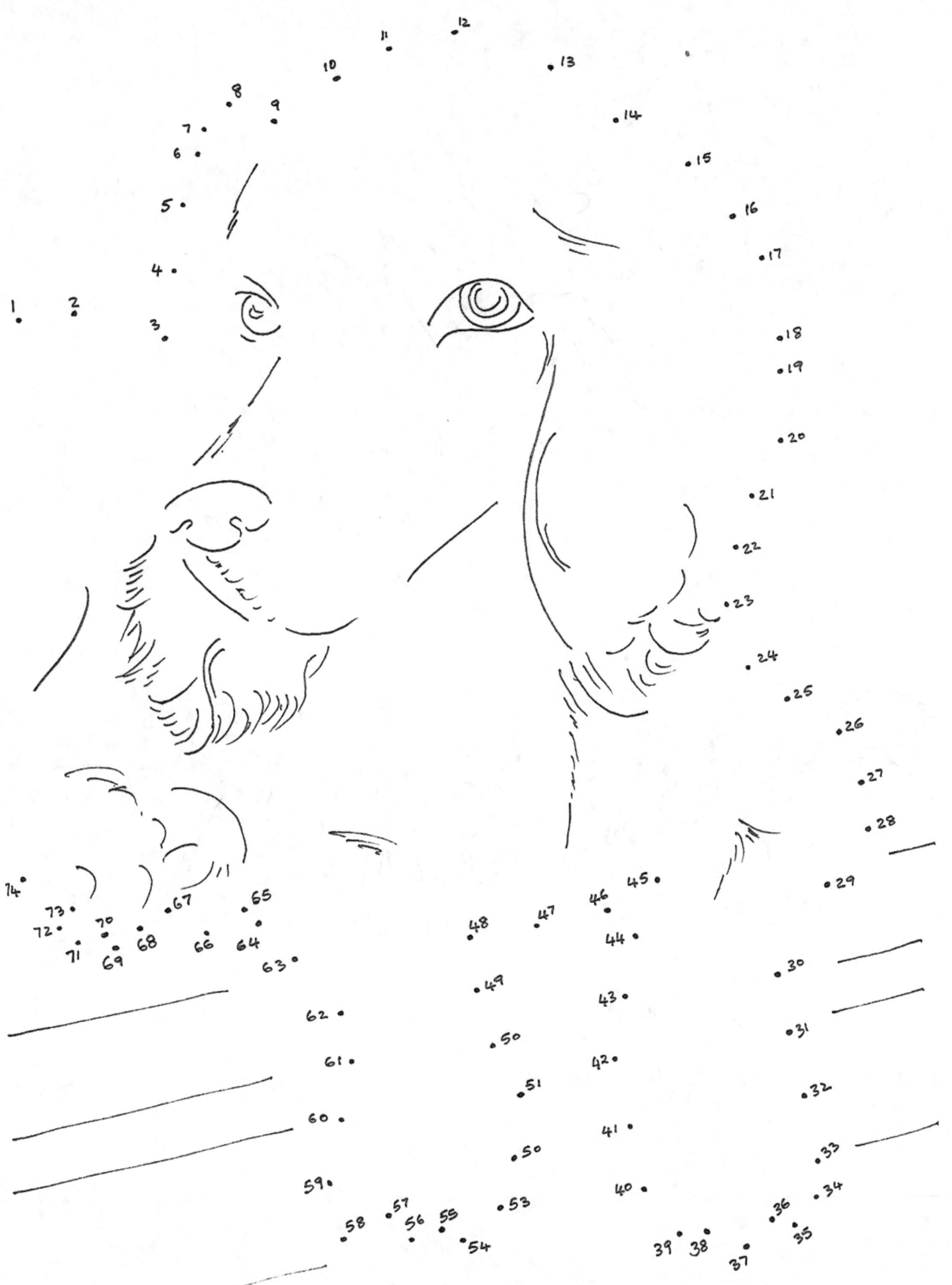

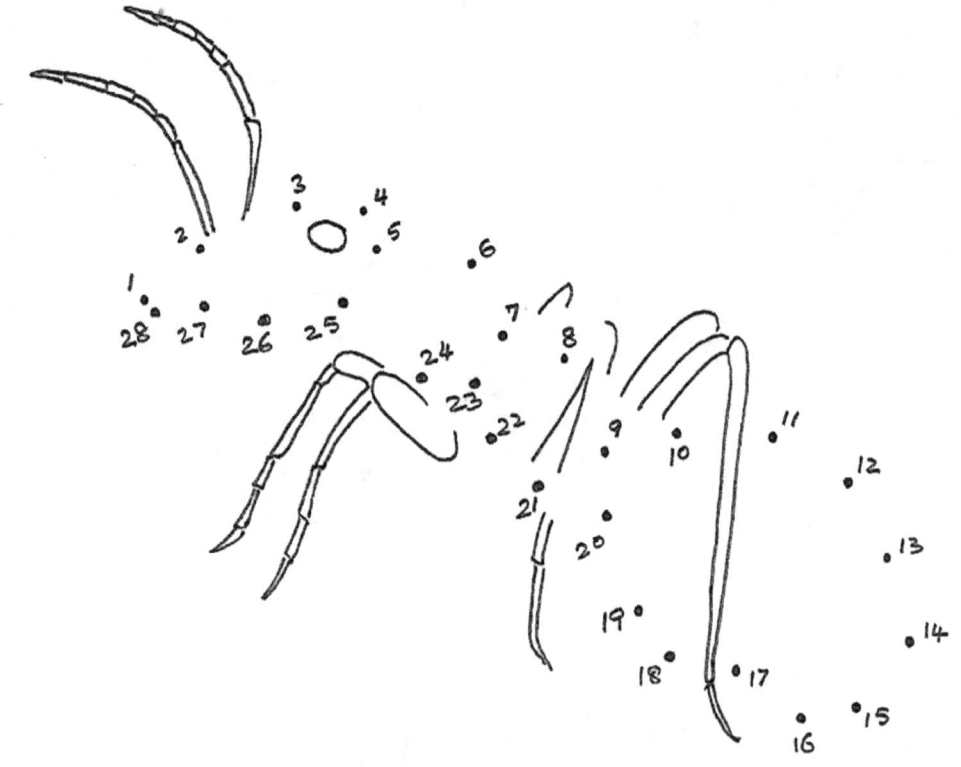
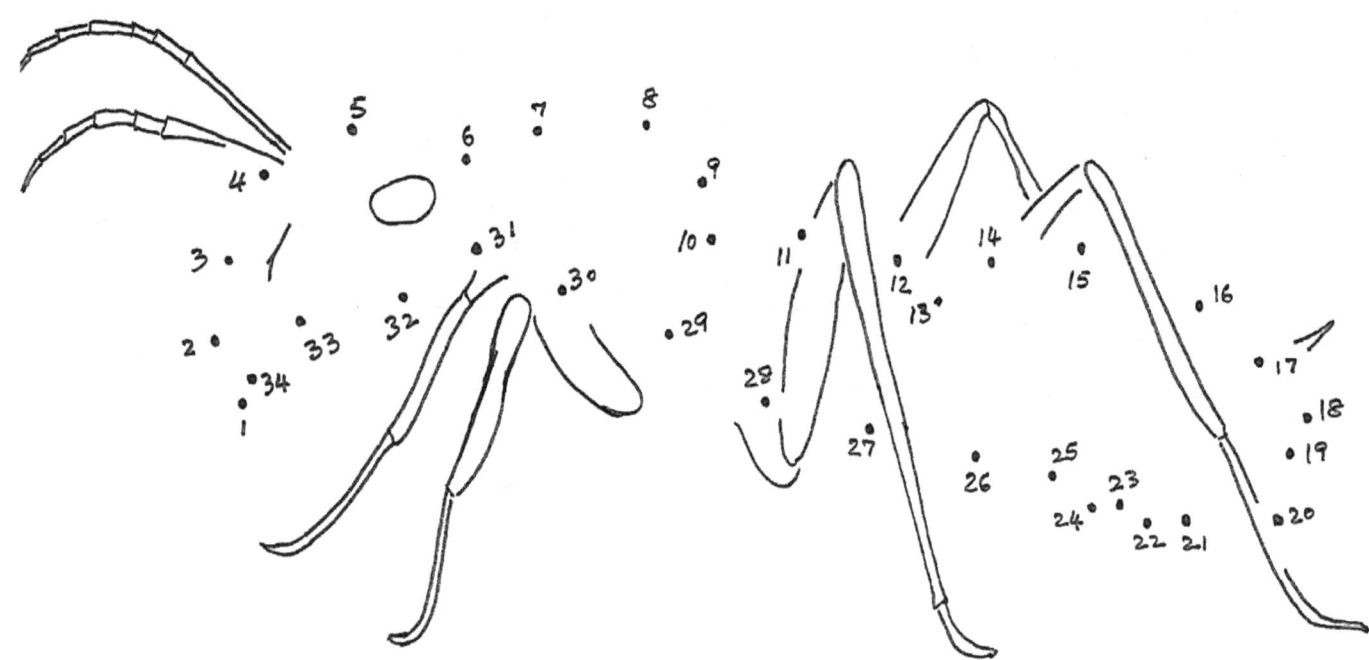

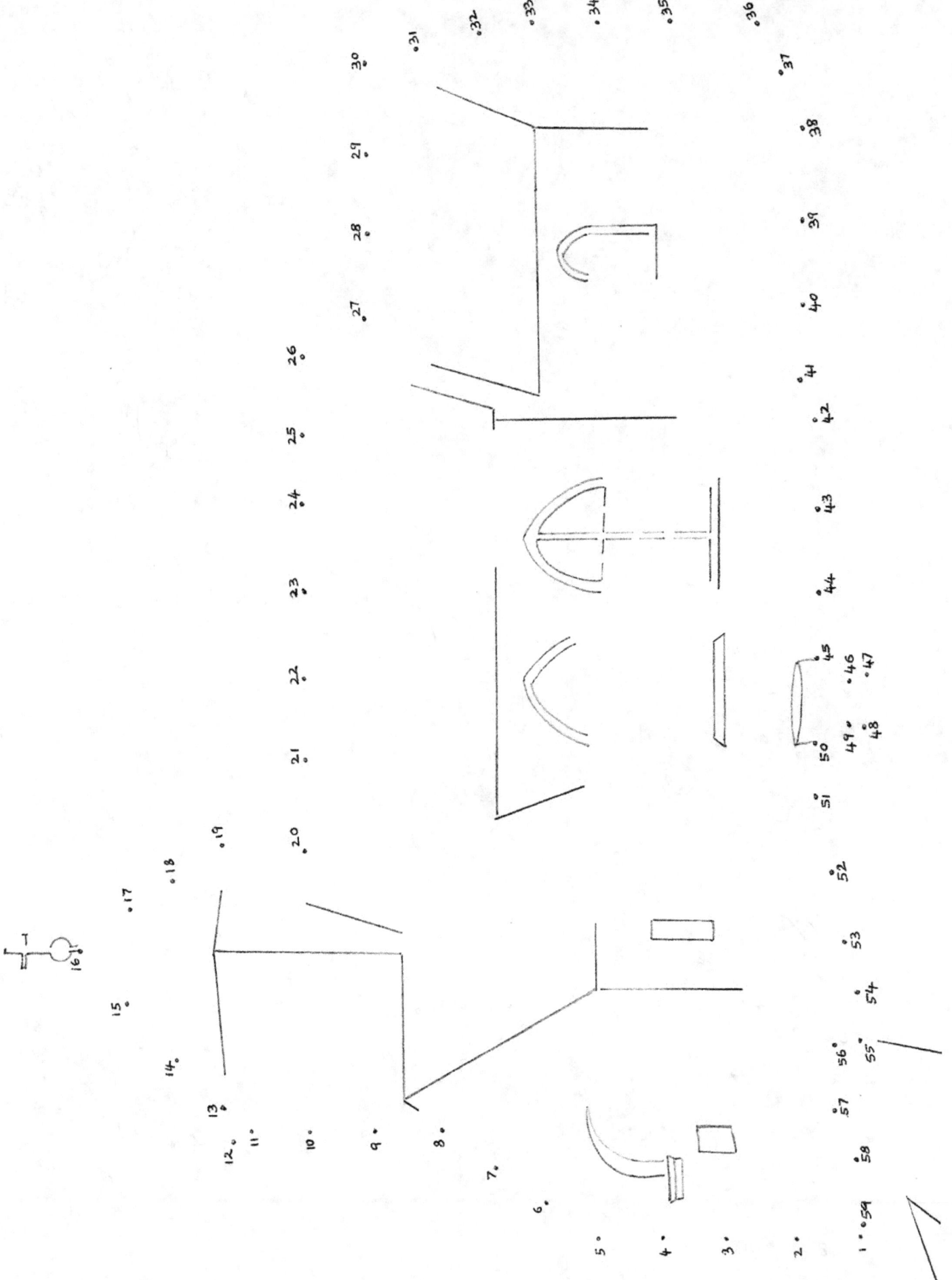

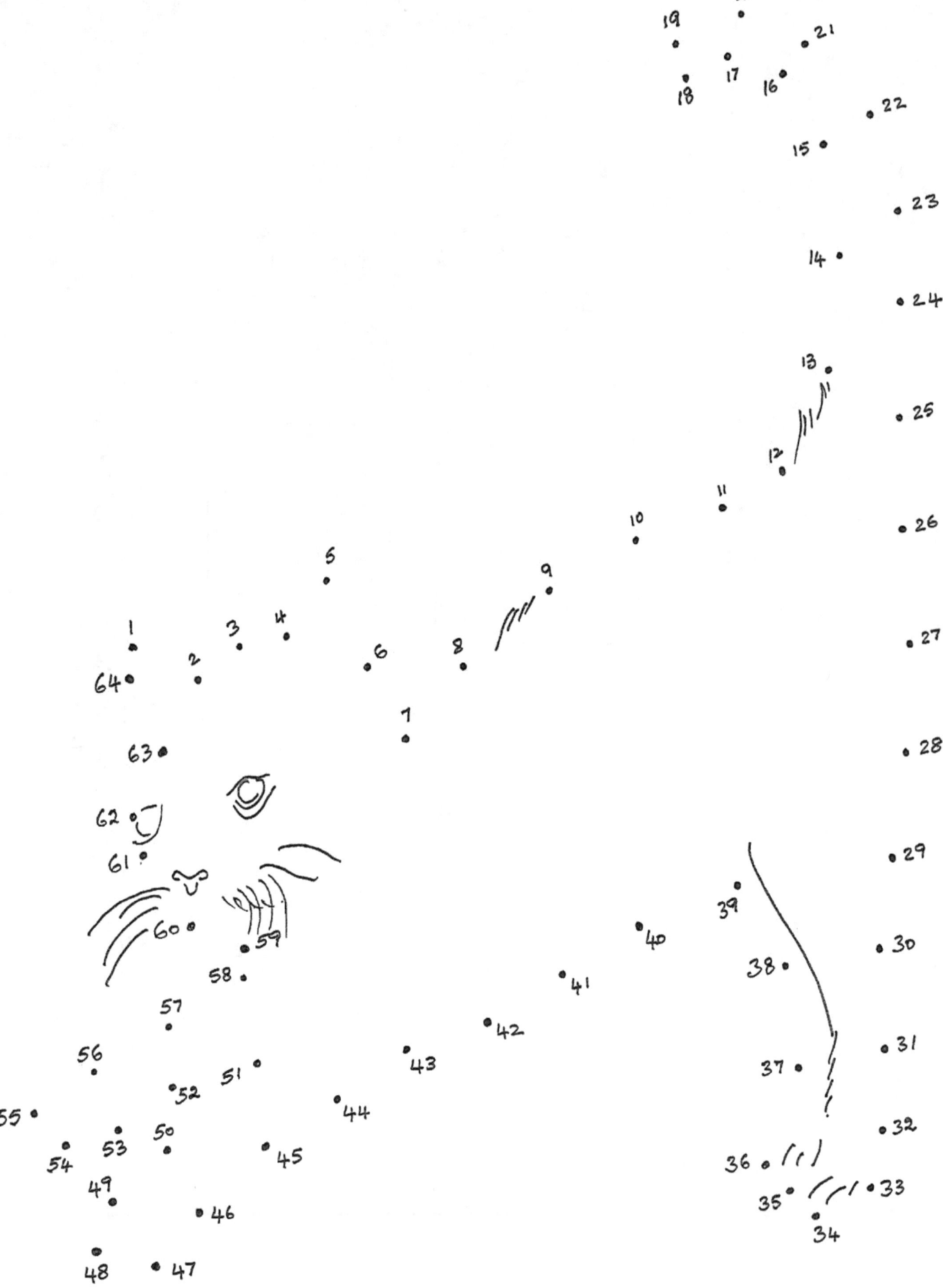

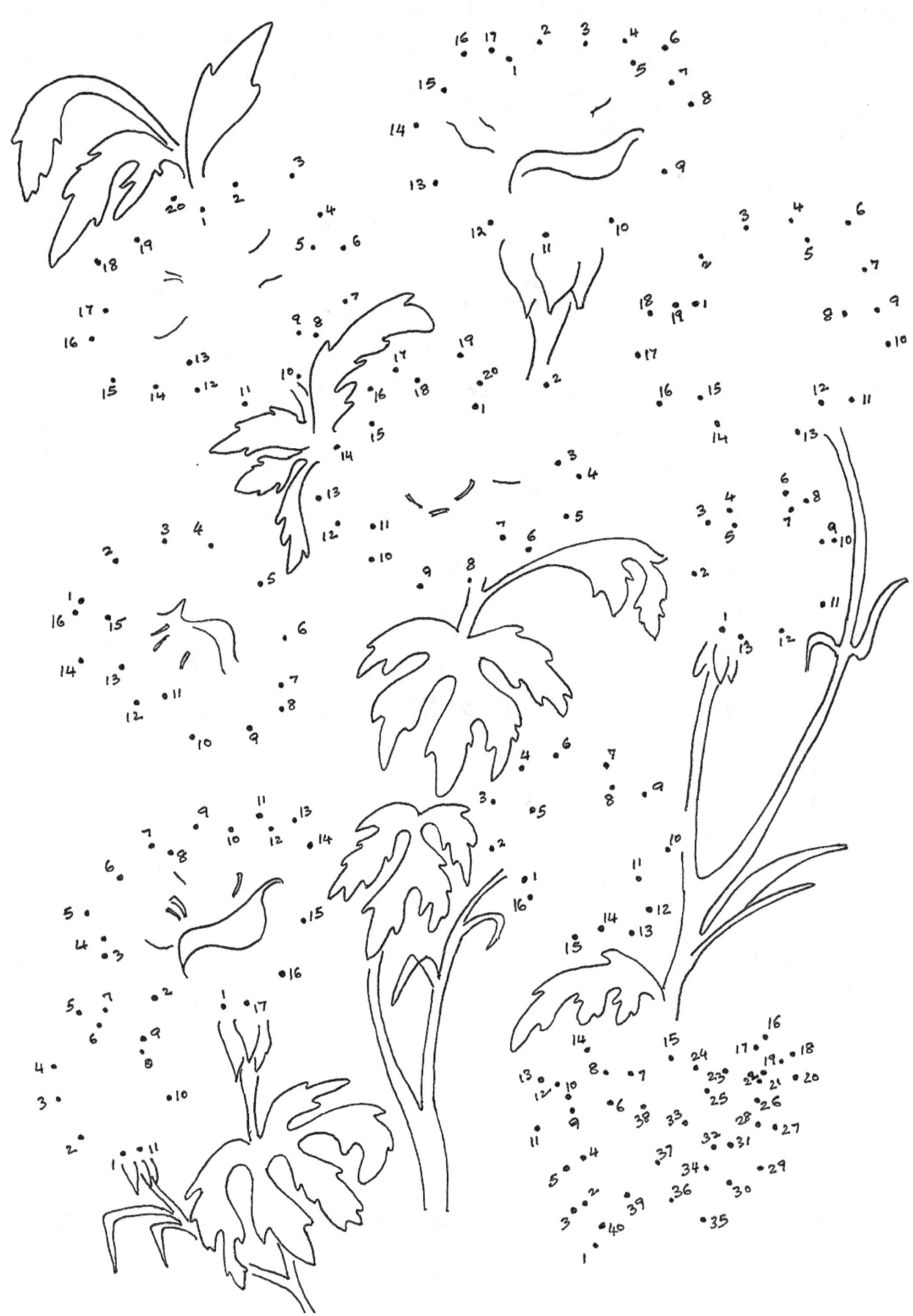

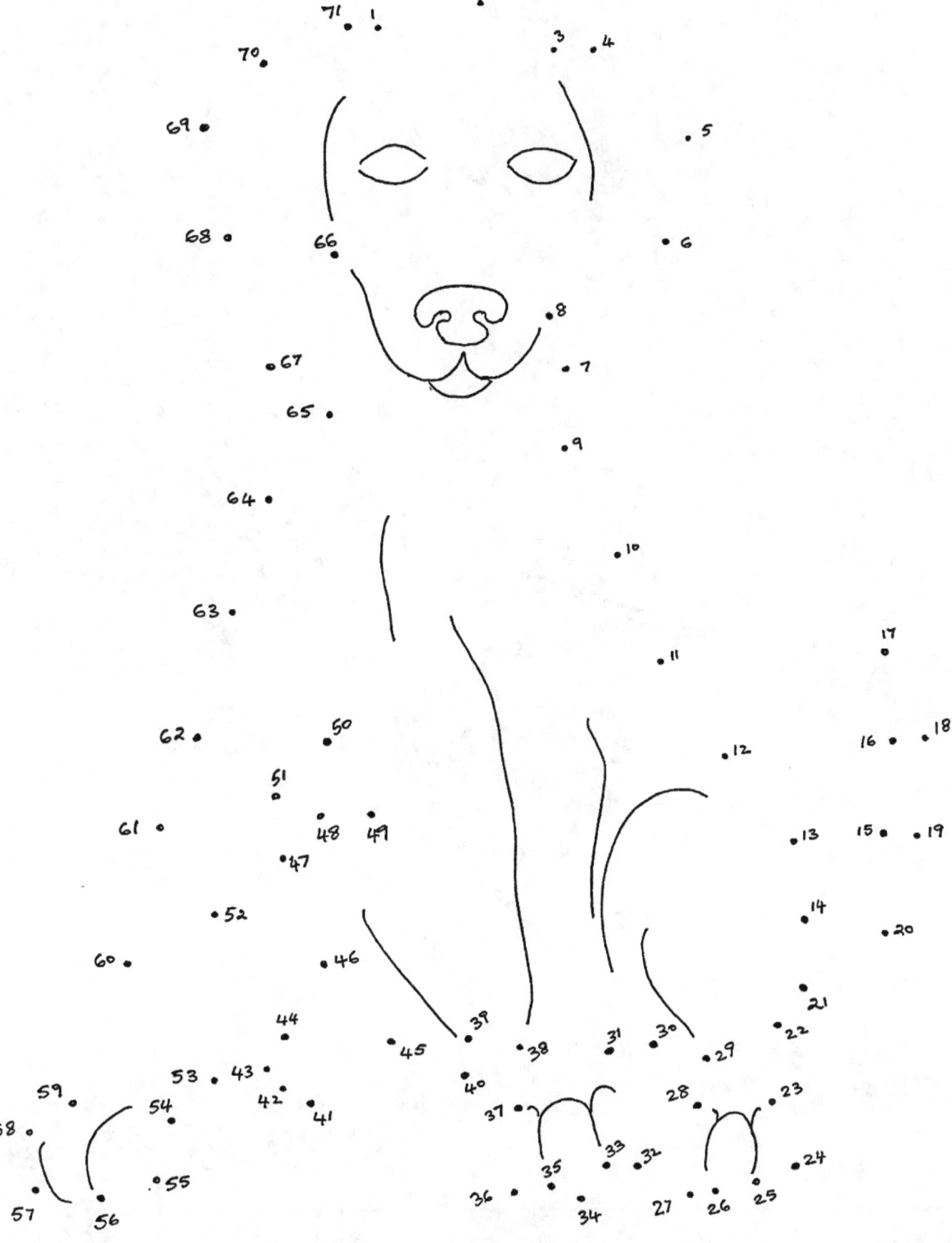

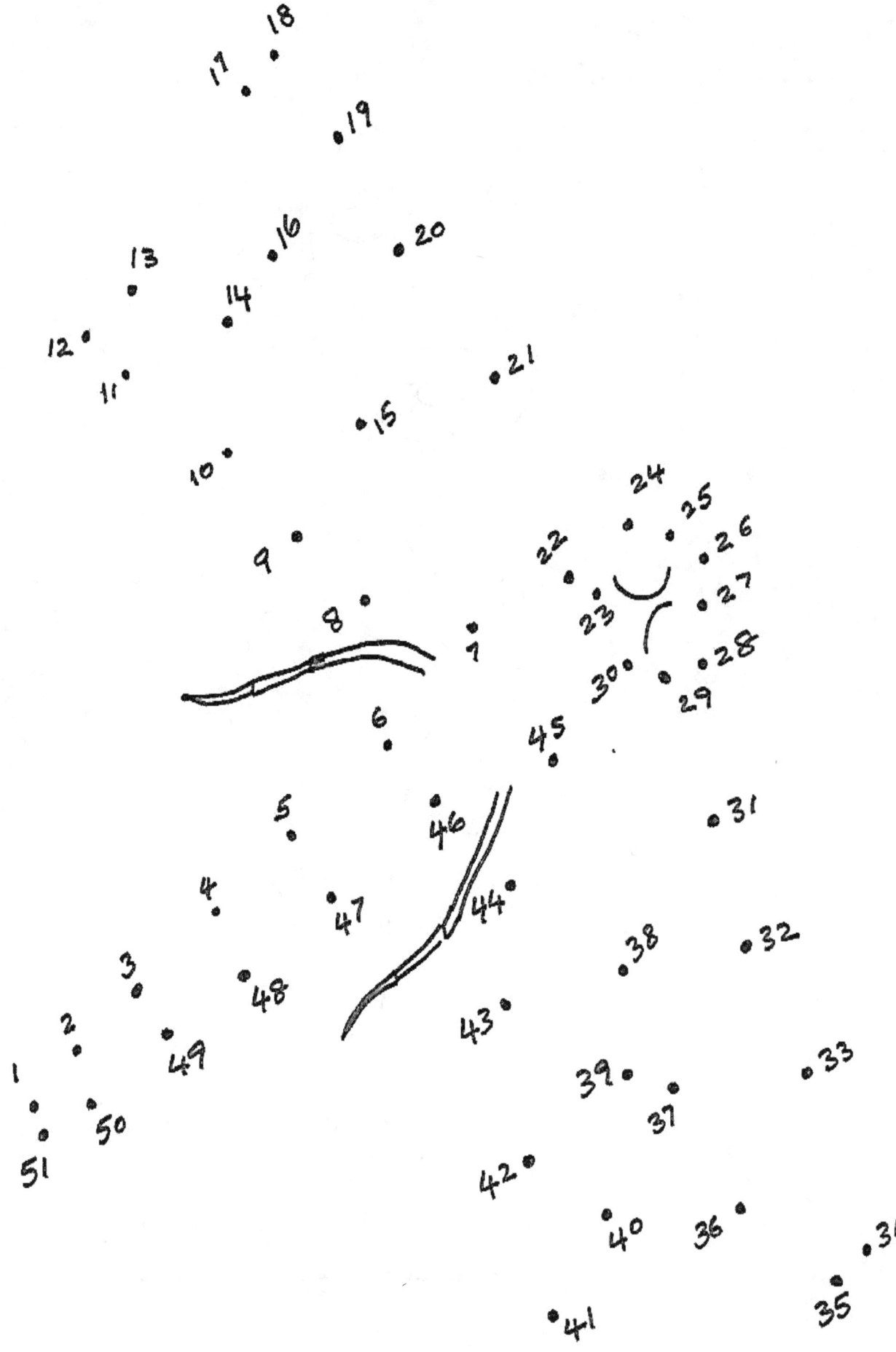

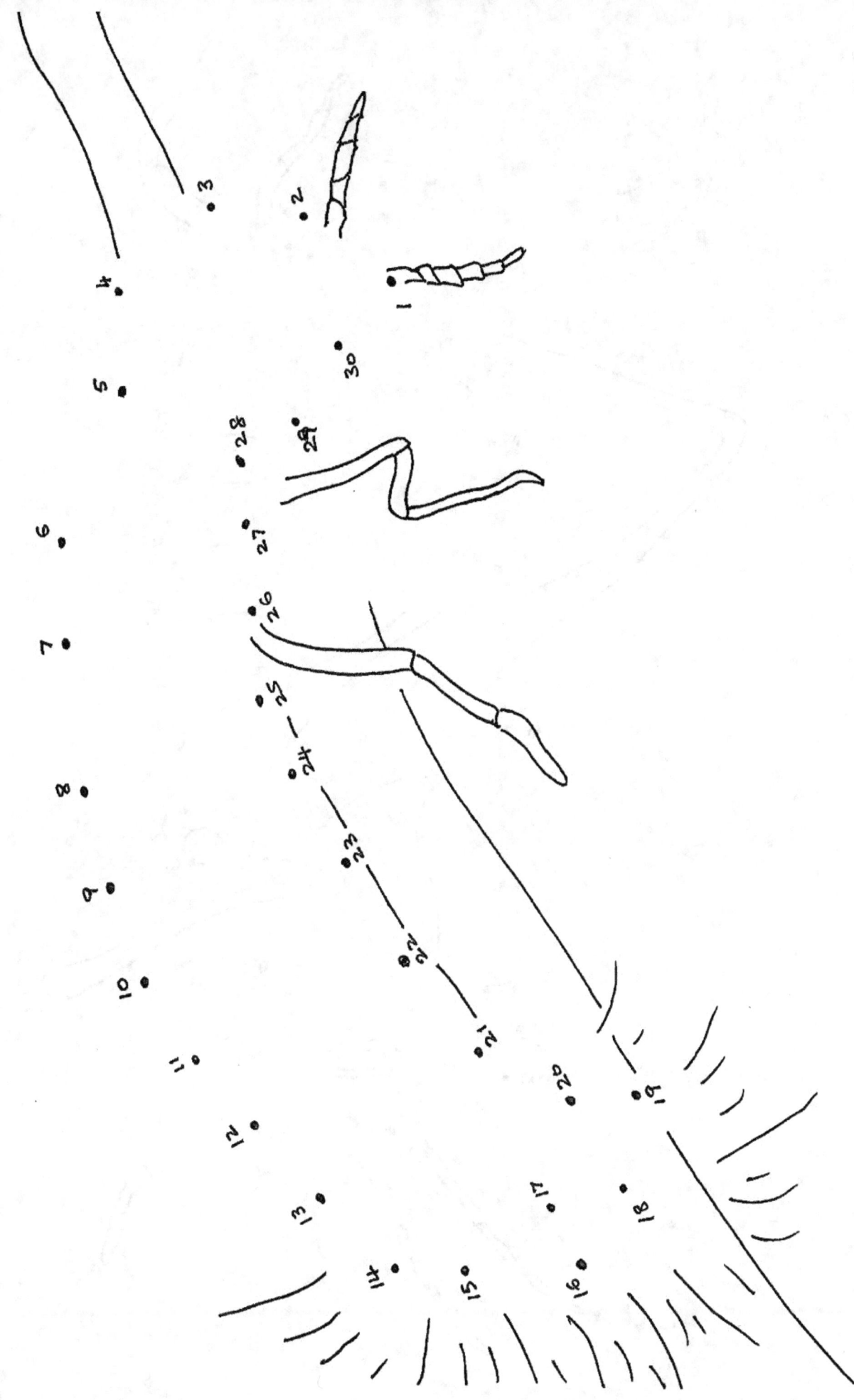

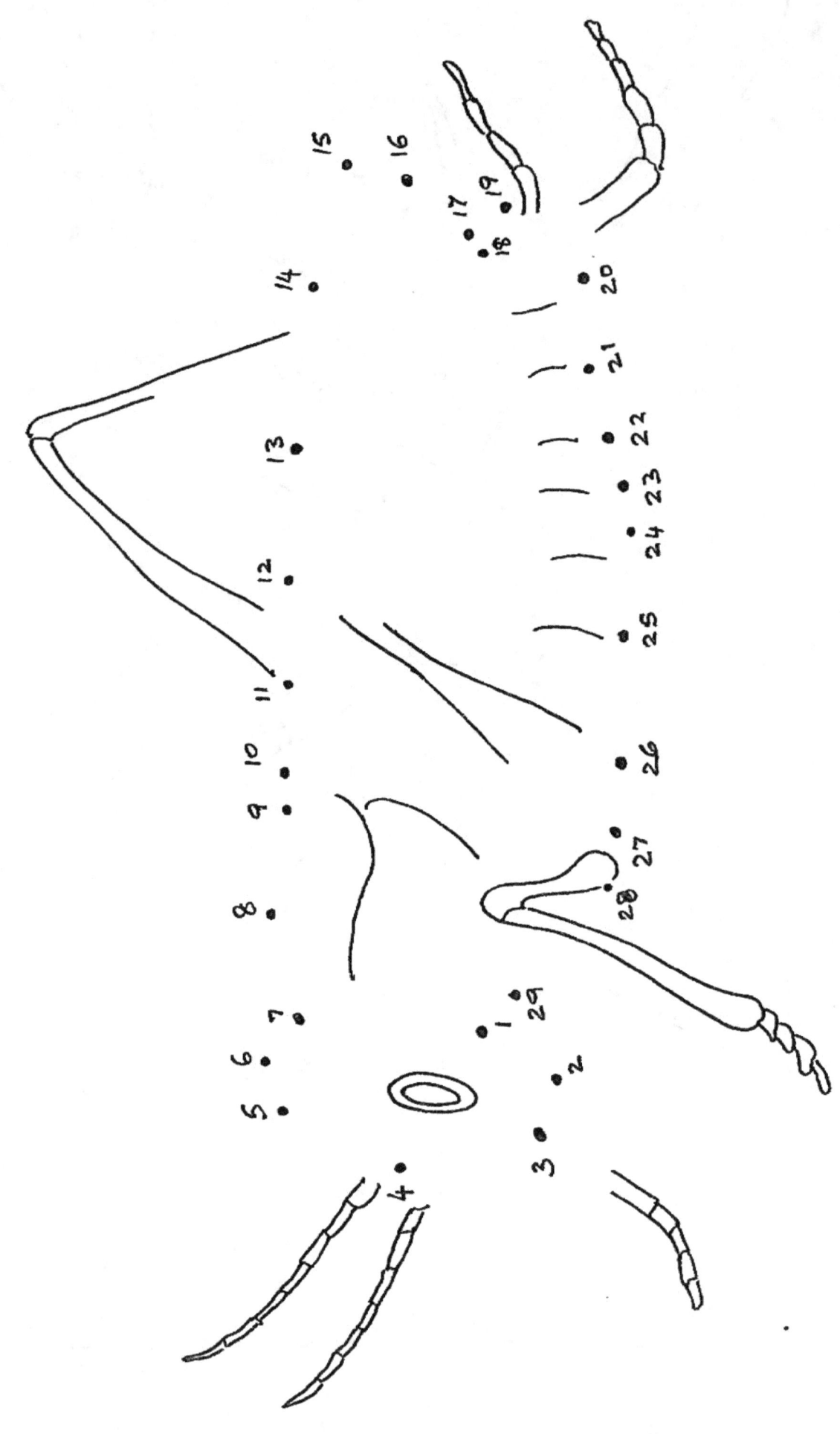

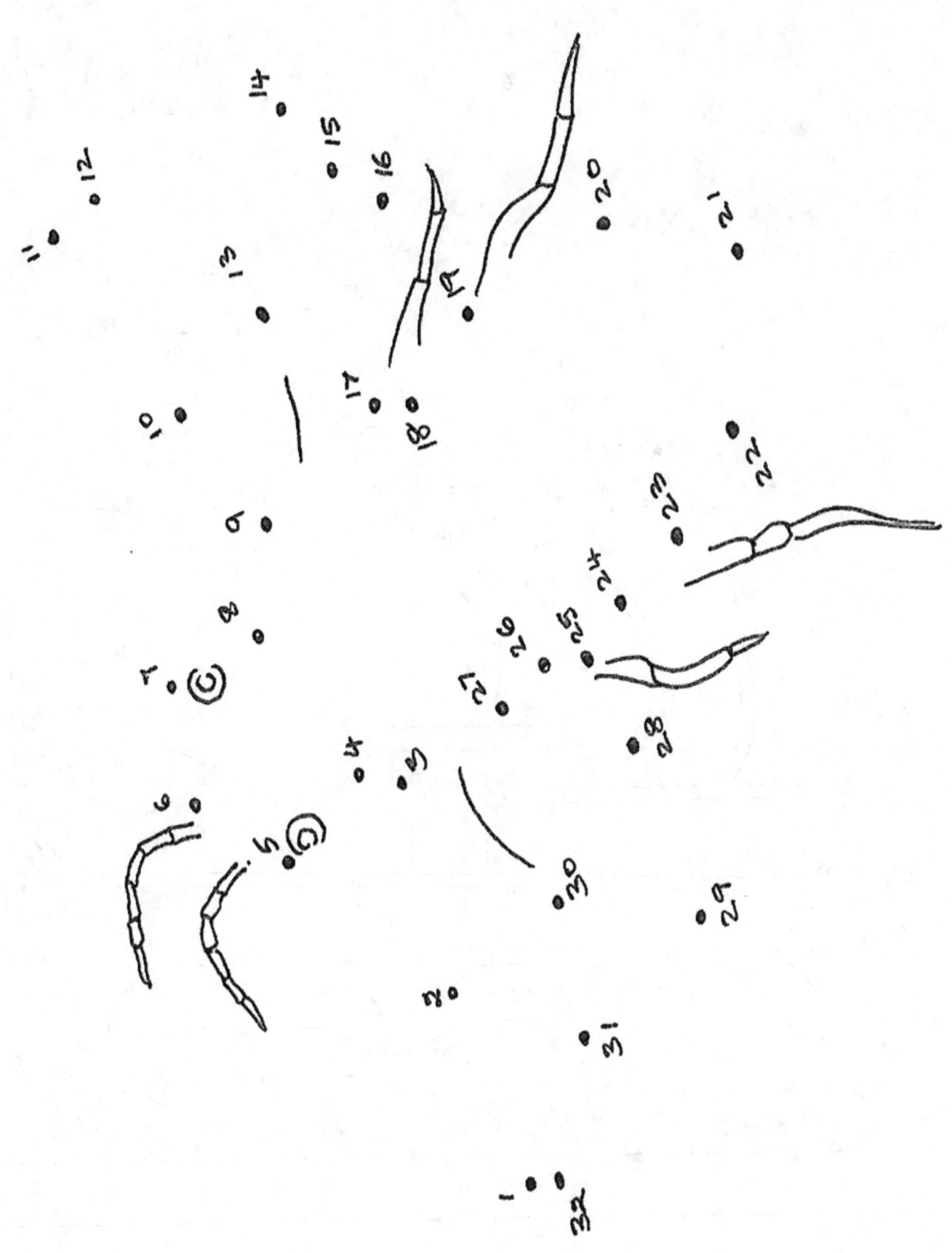

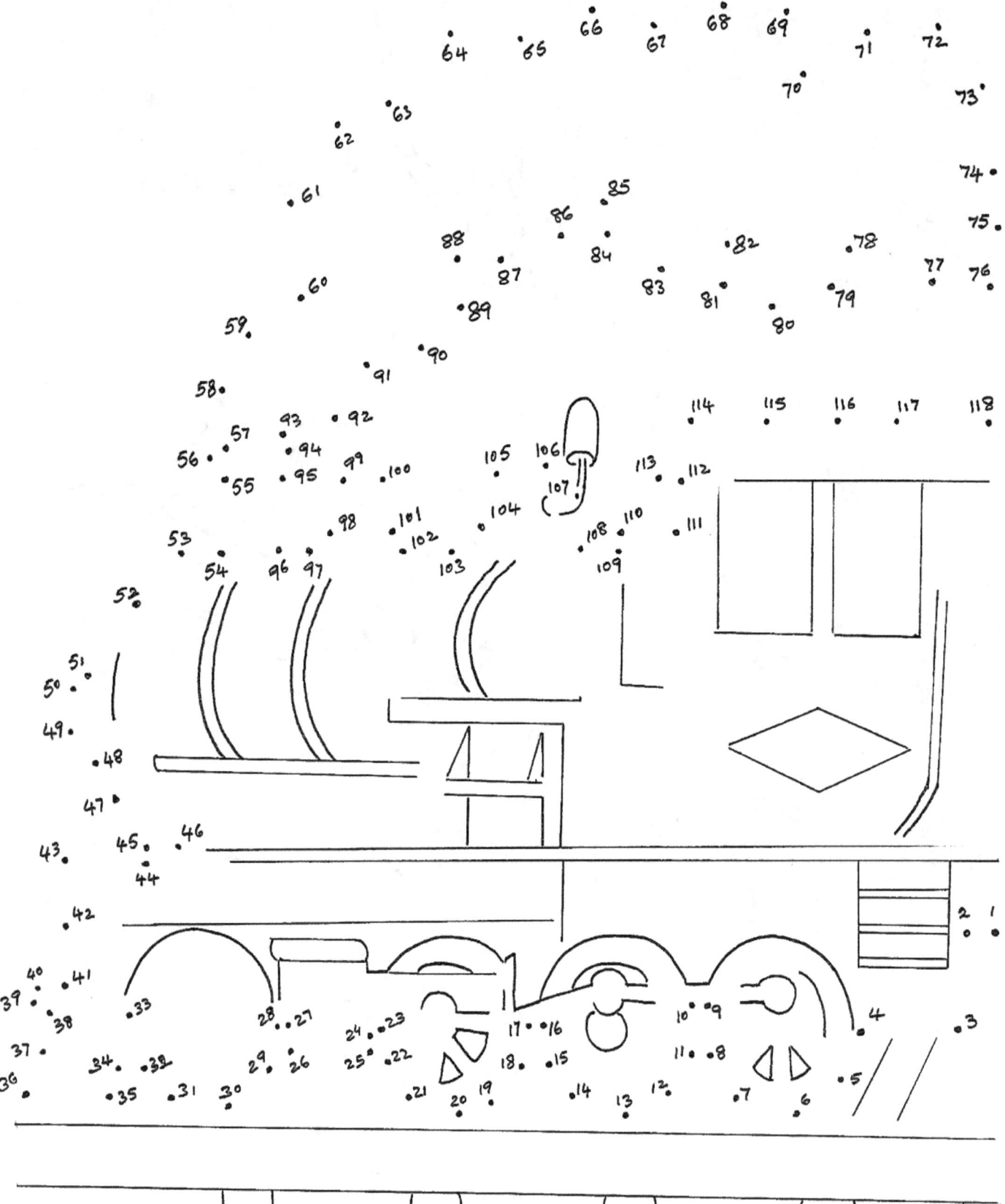

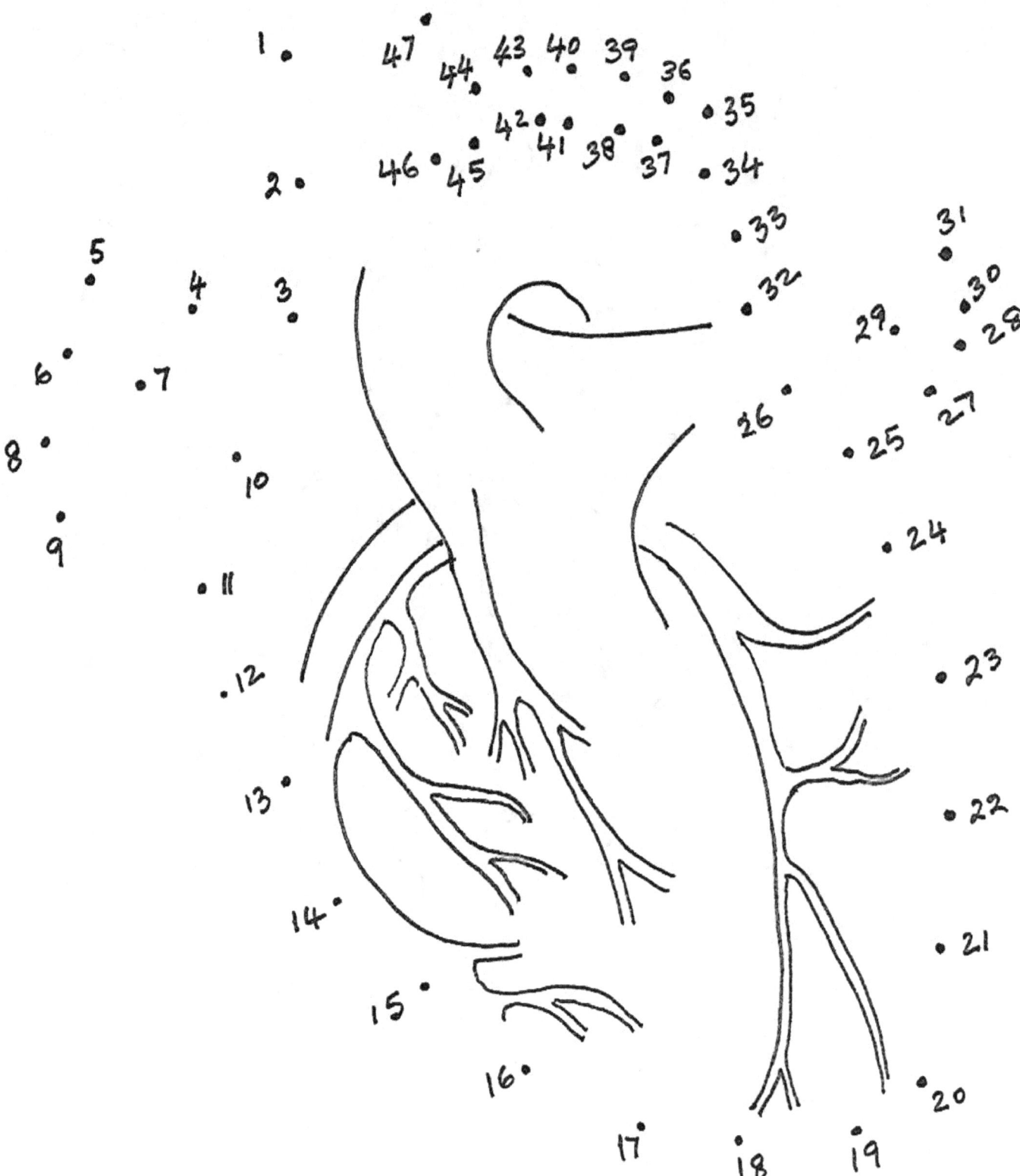

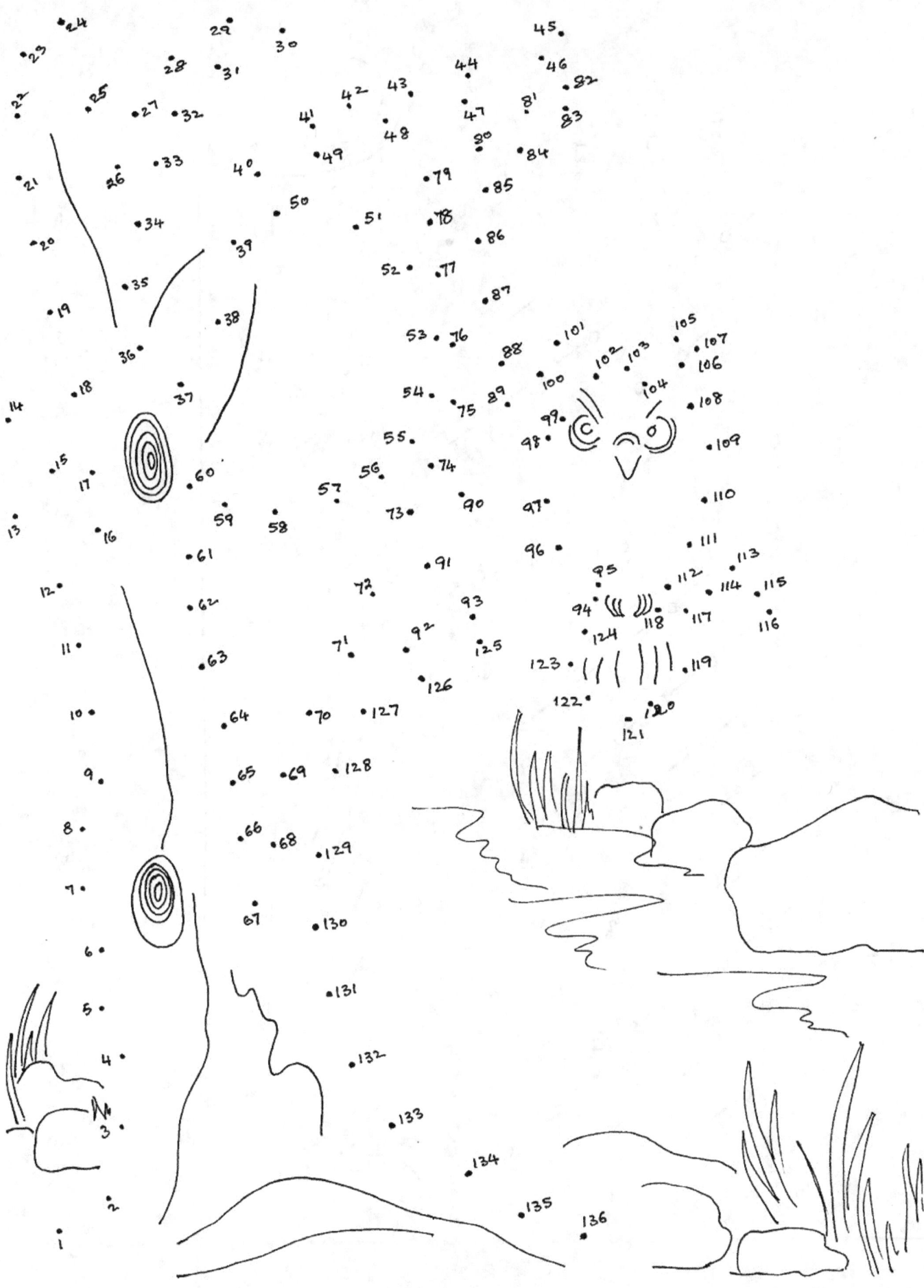

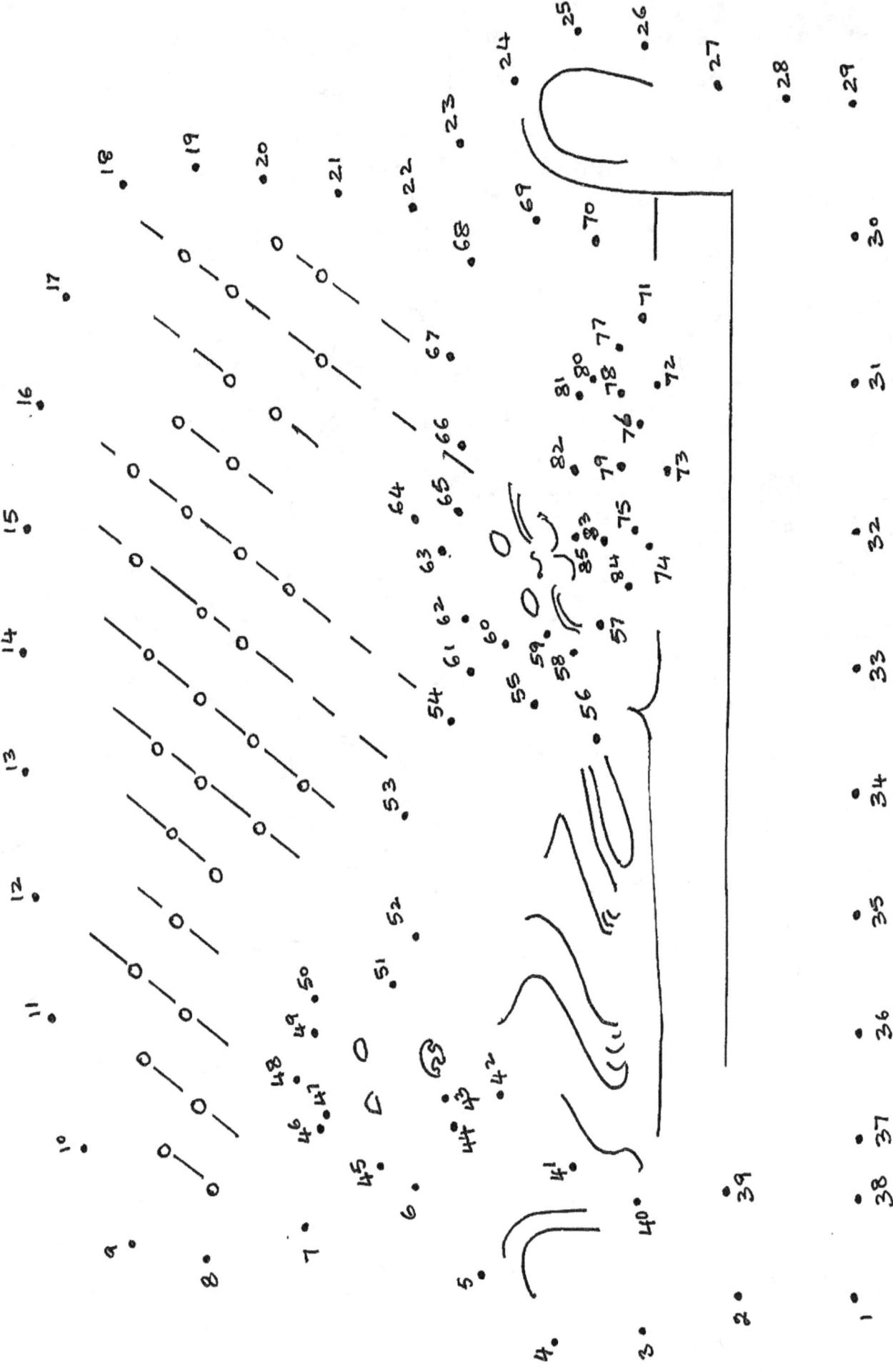

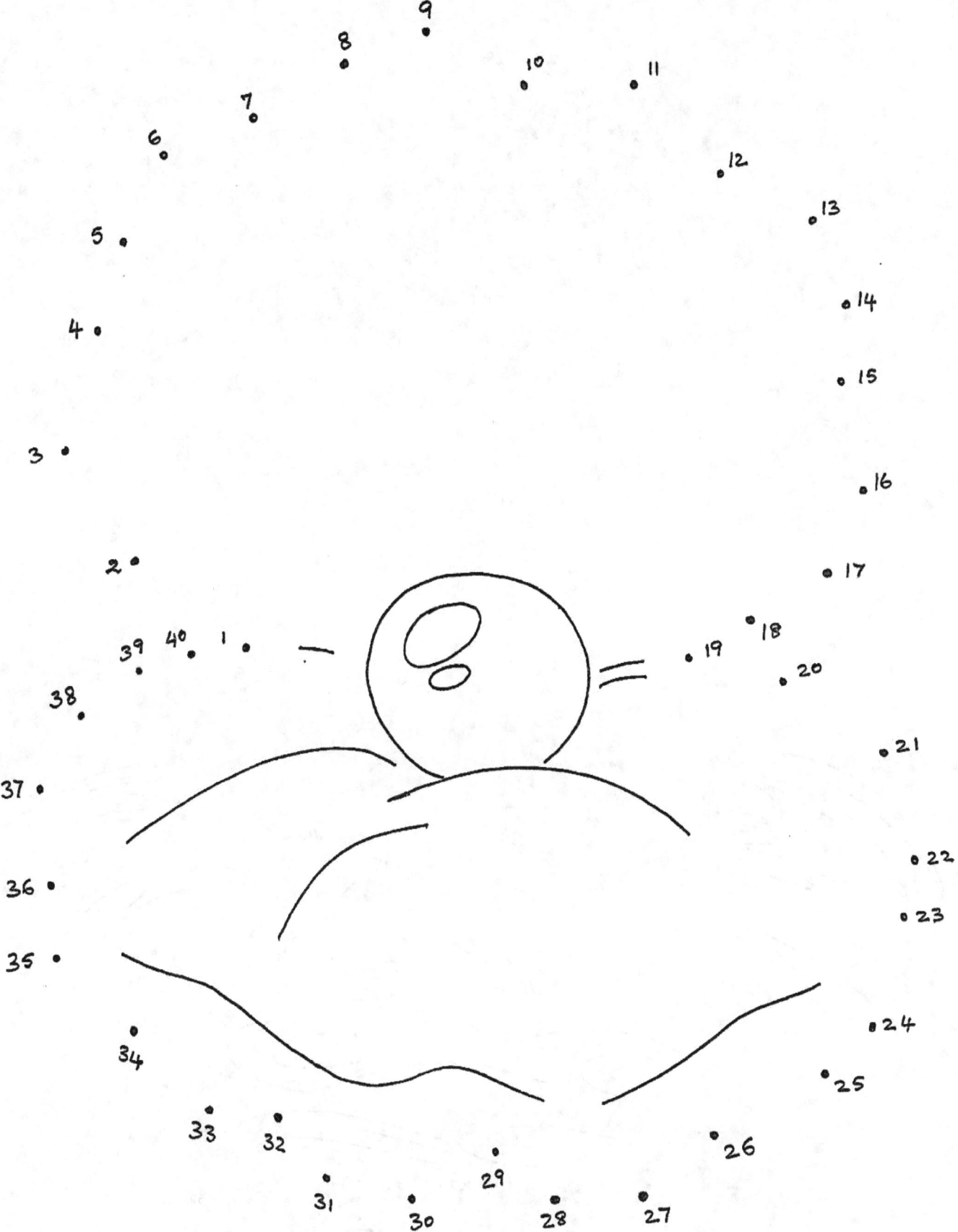

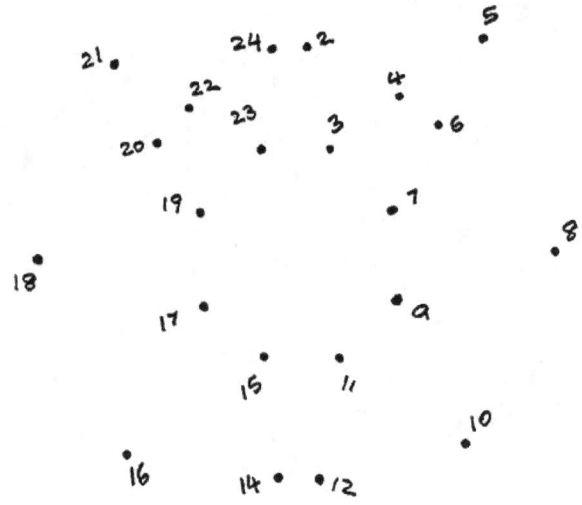

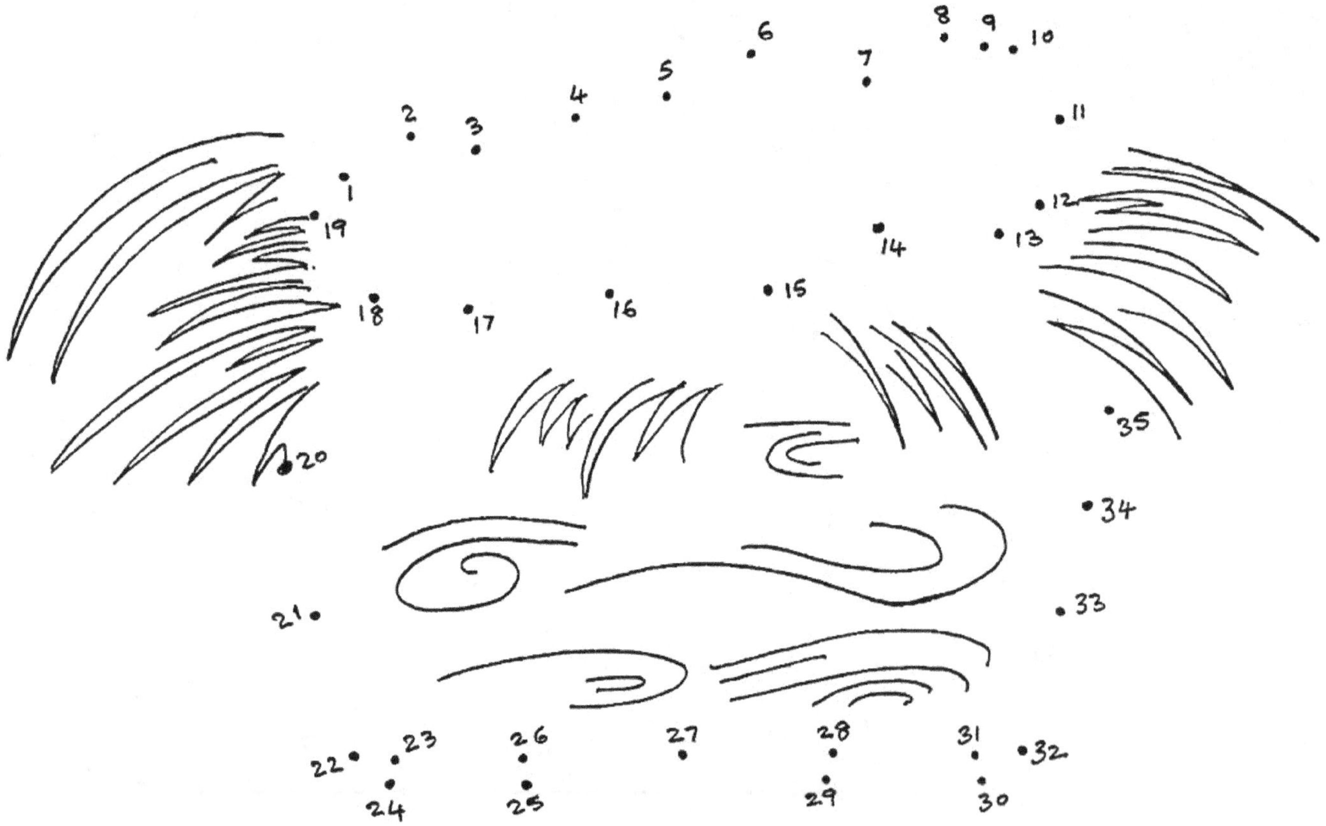

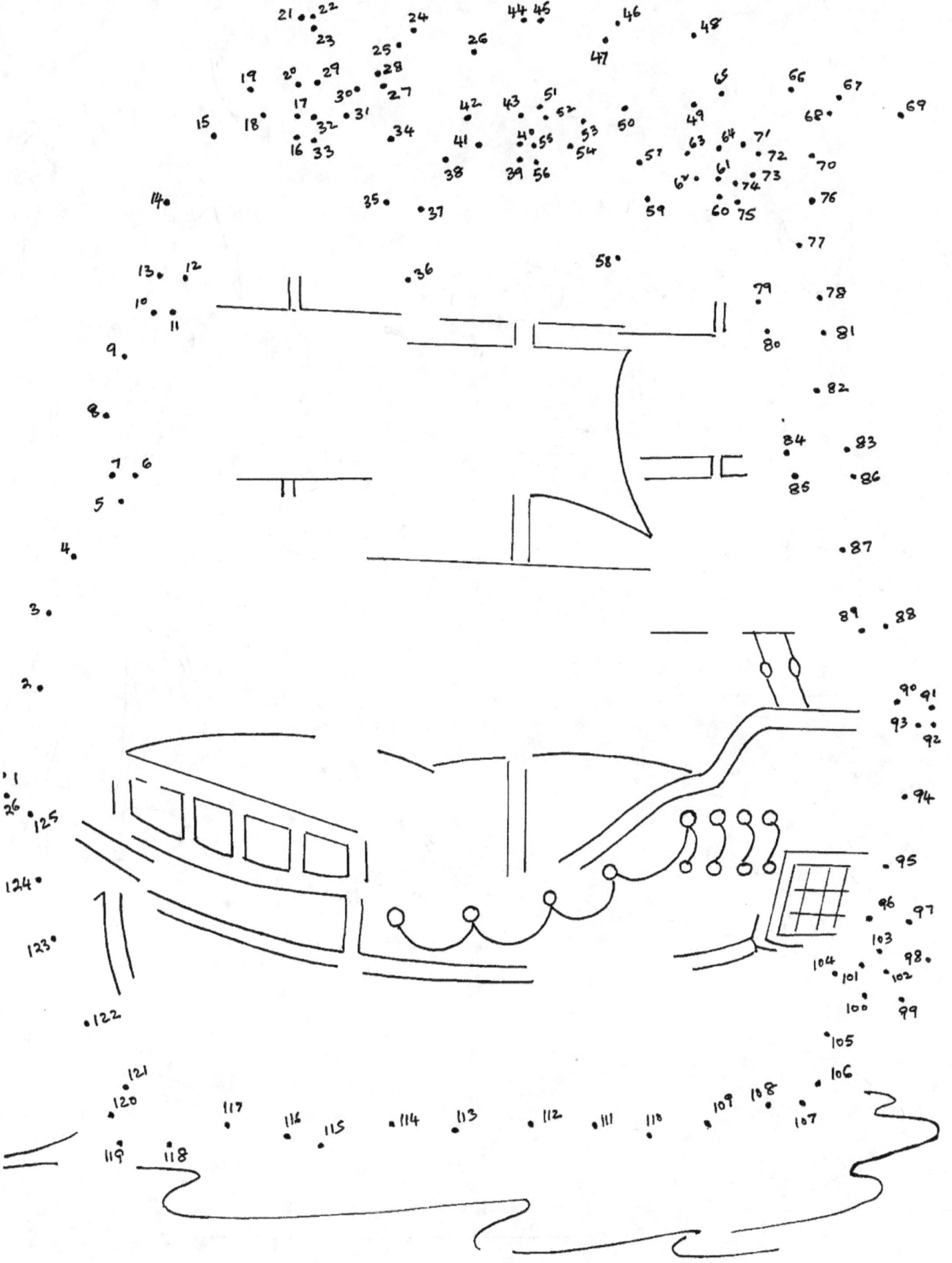

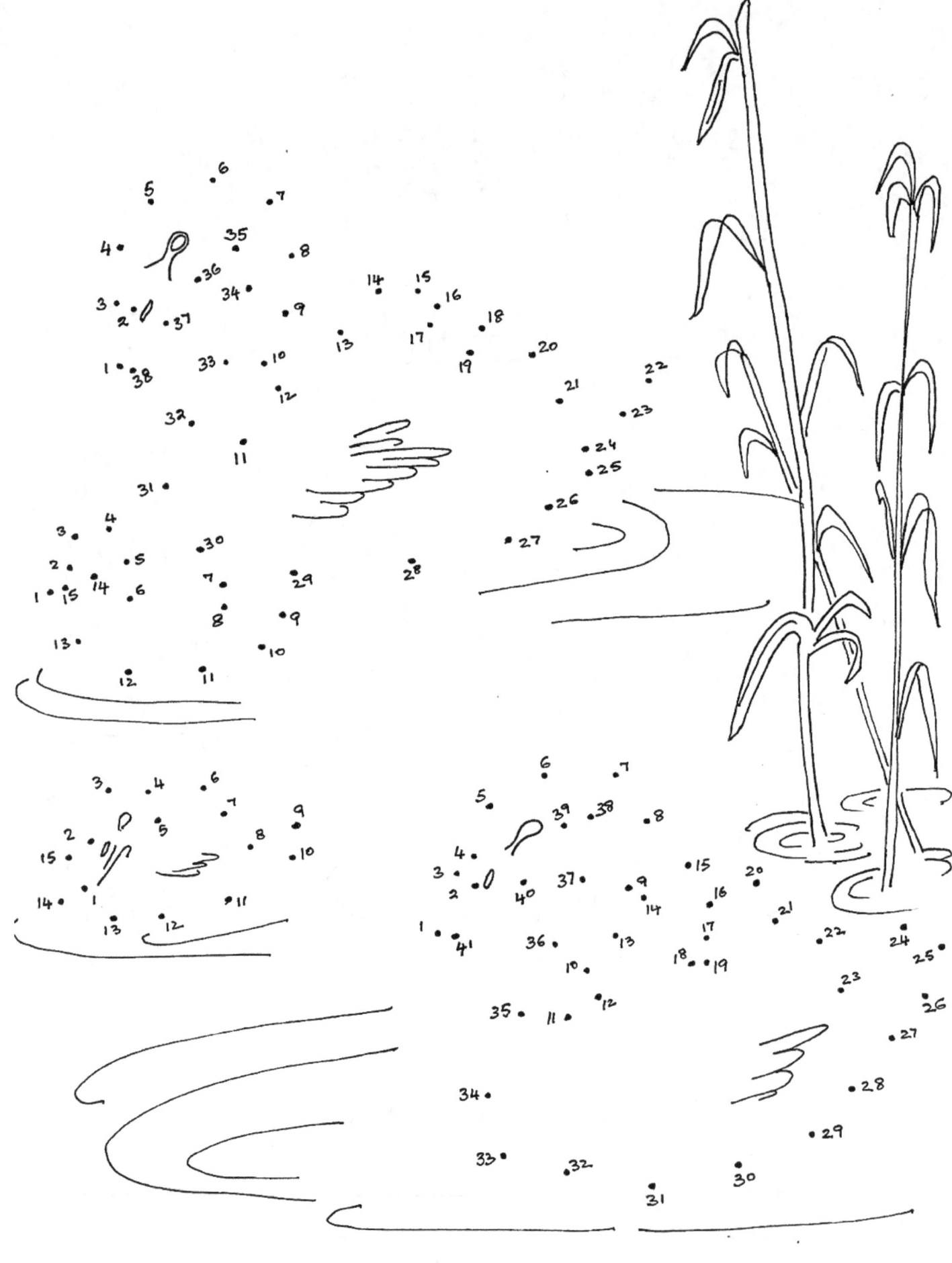

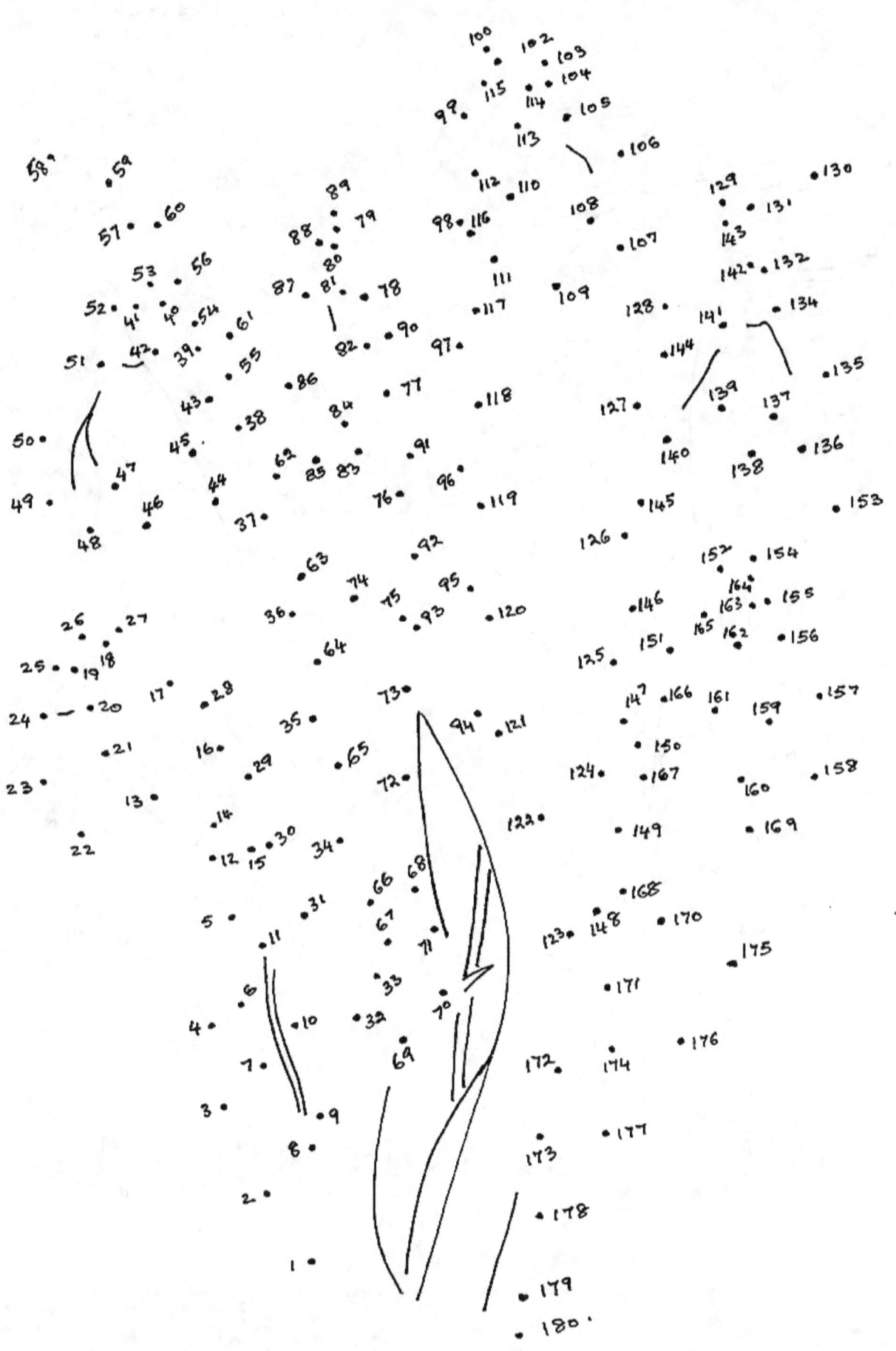

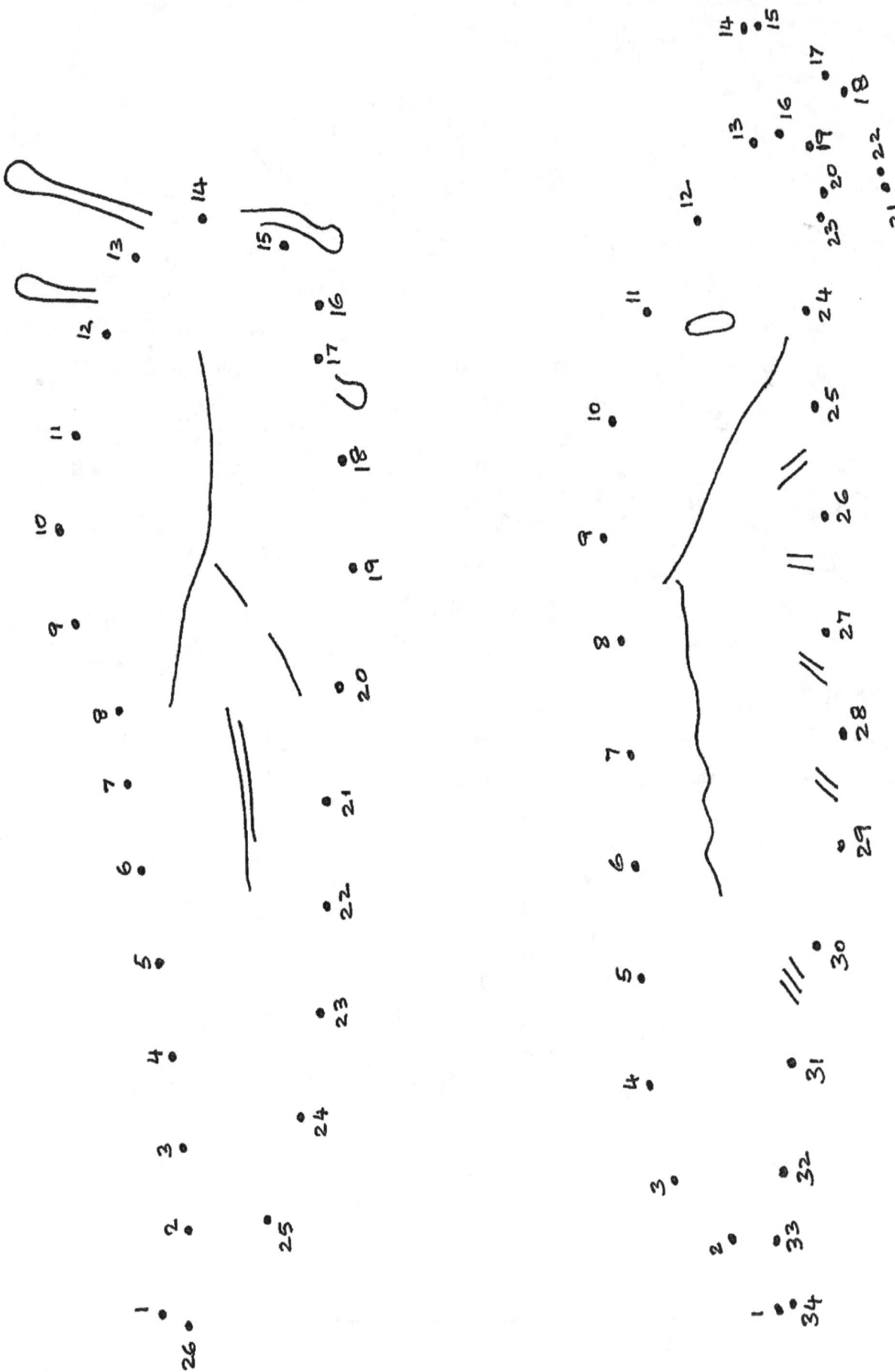

About The Author

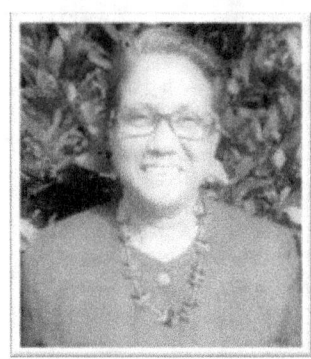

Ruth Irwin lives in Wiltshire, with her family. Born in India, she grew up in the Himalayan foothills. Raised by loving Christian parents, and taught from an early age to love God and walk in His paths; she has found love, hope, peace, joy and comfort in Jesus Christ.

All of Ruth's books encourage the reader to find strength and comfort in the love and grace of God. They offer hope and encouragement, reaffirming to the reader that we are God's most treasured possessions.

She has more poetry books to enjoy, for example: "ISHI" and "REVEALED IN POETRY AND PROSE". Both of these delightful books have colour pictures included within their pages for the reader to enjoy alongside the poems. Ruth has also authored 'YOU, A SPIRITUAL BEING' and 'STAYING CONNECTED TO GOD' to bless and encourage, and share God's love.

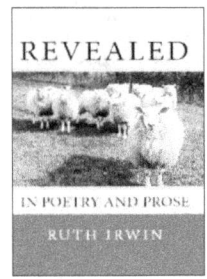 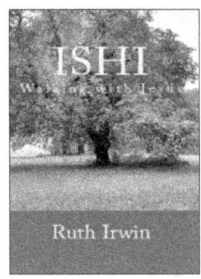 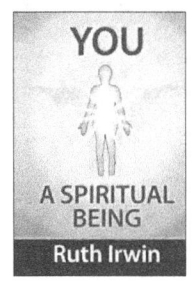 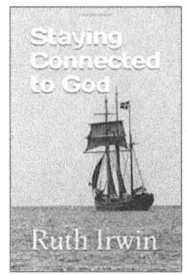

All are available at AMAZON (as well as many other online bookstores)